Heirloom

An Introduction to Collecting Antiques

Heirloom

An Introduction to Collecting Antiques

Edited by John Bly

ANGLIA
Television Limited

Boxtree

ACKNOWLEDGEMENTS

The publishers would like to thank the following for kindly allowing us to reproduce photographs
in this book:

Anglia Television Limited pages 6 and 7;
John Bly pages 89, 91, 92, 93, 94, 95, 96, 97, 98 and 99;
Brand Inglis pages 68, 69, 70, 71, 72, 73, 74 and 75;
Christies pages 124, 125, 126, 127, 130 and 131;
David Mason pages 79, 80, 81, 82, 83, 84, 85, 86, 87 and 88;
Phillips (London) pages 9 (above) 11, 13, 17, 20, 24, 27, 123, 124, 128 and 129;
Phillips (Exeter) page 21 and 23; Phillips (Scotland) page 30;
Henry Sandon page 9 (below);
John Sandon page 26;
Sotheby's pages 12 (left), 32, 33, 34, 35, 37, 38, 41, 42, 43, 45, 47
(left and right), 48 (top left and right), 48 (below), 49, 50
(left and right), 51, 54, 55, 56, 57, 58, 60, 61 (below), 62, 63, 64, 65, 66,
101, 102, 104, 105, 106, 107, 108, 109, 111, 112, 113, 114, 115, 116, 117, 118, 119, 120 and 121.
Worcester Royal Porcelain Company Limited page 18.

First published in Great Britain in 1989 by Boxtree Limited

Designed by Design Group, Bournemouth
Typeset by York House Typographic Ltd
Origination by Gilchrist Bros., Leeds
Printed in Spain by Cayfosa Industria Grafica, Barcelona

for Boxtree Limited
36 Tavistock Street
London WC2E 7PB

British Library Cataloguing in Publication Data
Heirloom: an introduction to collecting antiques.
    1. Antiques. Collecting
    I. Bly, John
745.1′075

ISBN 1-85283-246-0

CONTENTS

FOREWORD

Heirloom started transmission on Anglia Television in the early 1970s as an eight-minute item in the news magazine programme *About Anglia*. Over the years the interest and popularity that it engendered, mainly because of its presenter John Bly, demanded that it should become a programme in its own right.

Thus the half-hour *Heirloom* programmes started, and in 1985 transmission was extended from the Anglia region to the whole of Great Britain. Since then it has achieved a position in the national top 100 viewing figures – the only 'home grown' afternoon programme to do so – and throughout its last 13-week run gained such a high audience appreciation figure that it was the No. 1 show in the leisure and hobbies category every week.

The *Heirloom* approach of taking a single theme for each programme – porcelain, furniture, silver, etc. – endeavours to give the viewer a working knowledge of the subject whilst answering the all important questions of who made it, when was it made, where was it made, and yes, what's it worth.

When work on each new series begins extensive advertising through press and television brings in thousands of photographs from the public. It's only when these are sorted that the programme themes can be determined. Without this loyalty and enthusiasm from the viewers, we, quite frankly, would not have a series. But there are times when submissions are baffling; photographs such as those of a gentleman in a multi-coloured shirt, of modern washing machines and their owners, of numerous animals, and indeed quite a few children – all very nice to see but difficult to identify and value!

For me, one of the many delights of producing *Heirloom* has been meeting and working with some of the finest experts in the world of antiques. Within the programme theme, they are given complete freedom to bring along anything they wish to talk about. It is a pure joy to see the bravura approach they have for their particular subject – watch for instance David Mason cleaning a painting or Henry Sandon handling a piece of porcelain.

Over the years *Heirloom* has had its surprises. A bureau bookcase was valued at £20,000. One lucky viewer found himself the owner of a Holman seascape at £70,000, since sold to a museum in Los Angeles. But what is uppermost in the mind of the typical *Heirloom* participant and viewer is a desire to know, a need to know; and that's what *Heirloom* aims to do: enlighten, inform, and entertain.

Colin Eldred
Programme Producer

ENGLISH POTTERY & PORCELAIN

by Henry Sandon

Ceramics – the generic name given to items made of fused clays and stone – are the main items brought into the *Heirloom* programme and cover the whole gamut of collecting, from ordinary and common things to the rare and beautiful. As the subject covers such a huge range, I can do no more than touch on a few aspects that might give the reader a little understanding, enthusiasm to collect and warnings about some of the pitfalls. First, it might be useful to define the two types of ceramics – pottery and porcelain.

Pottery is basically opaque, that is, it is not translucent when held up to a strong light. The term not only applies to low-fired earthenware (clay) bodies but ranges up to high-fired stonewares made from specially fine clays. Low-fired pottery requires a glaze to make it watertight but stoneware will hold liquid without glazing although it *can* be glazed, for example with salt, to make it more attractive. Tin-glaze was used in an attempt to make the surface white and look like porcelain and is called faience, maiolica and delft.

Porcelain is translucent when held up to a light, but a lot depends on the thickness and firing of the piece – a pot that is very thick or underfired shows less translucency than a thin and well-fired one. The Chinese were the inventors of true (or hard paste) porcelain made from the two ingredients of china clay and china stone and fired at a very high temperature. The rest of the world was a long time behind China in making porcelain – Italy, France and England produced an artificial (or soft paste) body fired at a much lower temperature – although Germany made hard paste following its discovery by Meissen in about 1710. Bone china was an English development in soft paste porcelain in the late eighteenth century and this became the staple material in which the body had as much as 50 per cent of calcined ox bones, which gave great strength, whiteness and translucence.

BRIEF HISTORY OF ENGLISH POTTERY AND PORCELAIN

Early English pottery can be seen at its finest and most robust in the slipwares of the seventeenth century, slip being a liquid clay of one colour contrasting with the body of another colour. The great centres of production were Wrotham in Kent, and Staffordshire. Delftware of the seventeenth and eighteenth centuries was an attempt to make earthenware look like porcelain by coating it with a white tin-glaze. Main centres of production were London, Bristol and Liverpool but delft's failing was that it was not suitable for hot liquids. Much more practical wares were the red stonewares and saltglaze of the eighteenth century, the development of the finer earthenware bodies of creamware and pearlware by Josiah Wedgwood and others in the second half of the century, and the so-called Ironstone bodies of the nineteenth century. The growth of Staffordshire as a centre with larger and larger factories led to a growing industrialisation in the nineteenth century with transfer printing taking over from hand-painting. By the end of the century, lithographic printing in full colour was introduced and, apart from a fight back of simple hand-decorating in the Art Deco period of the 1920s–1930s by such designers as Clarice Cliff, lithos now rule.

English porcelain made in the mid-eighteenth century was mainly of the soft paste or artificial type, with such great firms as Chelsea, Bow, Derby and Worcester having their own formulas of different types of stone and clay. The discovery of the materials used in hard paste (or true porcelain) of china clay and china stone led to attempts at Plymouth and Bristol to make porcelain like the Chinese and Germans and this was followed by a number of firms such as Newhall, Coalport and Chamberlain at Worcester. The invention of bone china revolutionised Staffordshire and such firms as Spode and Minton became very important, but the finest porcelain of the first quarter of the nineteenth century was made in the old soft paste body by Flight Barr and Barr of Worcester, and a beautiful but difficult to make frit porcelain at Nantgarw and Swansea in Wales.

The only real rival to bone china, especially for ornamental objects, was Parian, which used a lot of feldspar and some cullet glass in the body so it could be left unglazed to simulate marble without becoming dirty. The first specialists in this were Minton and Copeland, who made superb

An interesting saltglazed teapot commemorating Admiral Vernon, who took Portobello in 1739 and Fort Chagre in the following year. The main panel is moulded with a three-quarter length portrait of the Admiral below the inscription 'Ad. Vernon/Fort Chagre'. The two remaining panels are moulded with the royal coat-of-arms. This rare teapot was sold for £3,300 at Phillips in 1985.

Large toasting mug in Nottingham saltglazed stoneware with a typical, shiny metallic glaze. It measures 15cm (6in) high and 13.5cm (5in) wide. An amusing inscription has been incised into the clay: 'William Smith, his cup 1777 and if it had been higher and wider it would have held more Toast and Cyder'. Bought many years ago for £5 when such things were not much appreciated; it is now worth £500.

An amusing tobacco jar in saltglaze stoneware by the Martin brothers, early twentieth century. Birds are the most expensive of the wares of the eccentric Martin brothers, a fine large example fetching several thousand pounds but many simpler pieces cost very little and should be looked for.

ornamental groups, figures and busts. Later Parian was glazed most successfully by Royal Worcester and Belleek, who still produce it. The 1860s saw the introduction of majolica, an attempt to look like Italian maiolica, the leading exponents of which were Minton, George Jones, Wedgwood and Worcester. This style was followed by Japanesque and the Arts and Crafts Movement of the 1870s mirrored in pottery by the Martin brothers and Doulton stoneware, Art Nouveau in the 1890s and Art Deco after the First World War. Limited editions came into their own after the Second World War and at their best, as in the horses and birds of Royal Worcester, were superb, but the production of huge amounts of lithographic printed wares has tended to swamp the limited edition porcelain market.

WHAT TO COLLECT

Now, what do you and should you collect? Most people have pieces that have descended to them from previous generations and these can often form the basis of a collection. These are the true heirlooms that can be passed on down to the generations to come. Perhaps they may not be very valuable pieces, not yet sought after by collectors, but I always enjoy the sense of pride and love with which the owners bring them into a recording of the *Heirloom* programme and talk about them. One problem here is that the pieces may not be to your taste at the time nor fit into your home too well, and it is certainly true that what one generation likes is often hated by the next. But persevere – a liking for it will often grow and it frequently happens that the next generation will worship the style again.

If you are starting a collection from scratch it can be fun to look for something that is not yet collected and therefore cheap. A couple of years ago, my wife started collecting small figures by the firm of Wade for her granddaughter to enjoy, play with and to form a collection. These simple, but charming pieces were all over the place, at prices of 35p upwards, but growing interest and the production of a book on the subject have made them much more collectable and prices for the rarer items have increased.

The work of our modern craftsmen potters can be both beautiful and, at the often ridiculously low prices asked, of practical use. Buy pots you like and you may well be supporting a rising star of the ceramic world. Some of the craftsmen potters of the last 60 years have already achieved fame and their work is expensive. From Bernard Leach, regarded as the 'father' of modern craftsmen potters to Michael Cardew, Lucie Rie and Hans Coper, the work is of

A pair of Staffordshire pottery portrait figures of cricketers, probably representing the batsman Julius Caesar and bowler George Parr. Sporting figures are among the most sought after of these Staffordshire figures but the novice should beware of the great numbers of reproductions of the cricketers and the prize fighters 'Heenan and Sayers'. The copies are usually very lightweight, often have large and regular crazing and are smaller than the originals, the ones illustrated being 35cm (13½in) and 36cm (14in) high. A genuine pair would be worth about £800, whereas a reproduction pair would only fetch about £30.

extraordinary beauty and strength, each piece a one-off. Find yourself younger potters of this quality, support them and enjoy their work, for these will be the heirlooms of the future.

There are many things of the present century that must be collectable. A fine collection can be made of the simple but attractive 'fairing' type of objects made by Goss, Willow Art and other potteries either side of the First World War. An enormous amount of this is available, mostly at just a couple of pounds or so per piece if it is common, but much more if rare. An interesting collection of wares commemorating royal and other events can be built up but if you want pieces earlier than Queen Victoria's Golden Jubilee you will have to pay quite a lot of money.

Other things that can be bought at auction very cheaply at the moment are modern limited editions. These can usually be found way under cost price and if you go for items of fine quality, like the horses and bulls modelled by Doris Lindner for Royal Worcester, or the same factory's birds modelled by Dorothy Doughty and James Alder, you will have porcelain of which you will be very proud. These can be found at a lower price than they have been for some years, as also can the many fine models made by rival firms in the 1970s and 1980s and ought to be good investments. However, the mass-produced plates and ornaments, tens of thousands of which are often made, generally do not constitute good short-term investments. Nowadays there are even fine artists who will do an individual plaque, vase or coffee service to your own requirements. Watch out for their work, which will be much less expensive than the factory-marked pieces of the established firms.

If you wish to collect something older, watch out at an auction or in antique shops for tea and dinner services of the nineteenth century. One of these will almost certainly cost you less than the price of a new service, but will have a greater amount of hand work in it. Also very much undervalued are the simple tea services of the turn of the eighteenth and nineteenth centuries, decorated just with hand-gilding or with a simple blue line and gilding. These can often be found at just a few pounds a piece and must be wonderful value. And at that price you could use them too! A general word of warning though: early pieces should be washed carefully in warm water with a gentle soap, not a detergent. *Never* put them into a dishwasher. Or why not start a collection of eighteenth-century Derby figures. Though not rare, these are very attractive and well

Left Copeland Parian figurine of a child cradling her pet dog, entitled 'Go To Sleep'. The typical Victorian sentimentality and the growing appreciation in Parian ware make this a desirably collectable object worth perhaps several hundred pounds.

Right A pottery Sunderland lustre jug, decorated with a coloured over-print of the great Sunderland bridge and, on the reverse, the Farmers Arms with the typical motto 'God Speed the Plough'. This piece is in a very fine condition for its date (very early nineteenth century) and sold at Lawrence's auctions in 1988 for £264.

made. In my opinion they are well worth looking out for, especially if in good condition.

The last few years have also seen large advances in value in many items that were too cheap at one time. Such items as Parian ware figures (white, unglazed porcelain of the 1840s to 1870s), Staffordshire pottery chimney ornaments and pairs of fireside spaniels, Toby jugs, Staffordshire slipware and saltglaze, almost all pre-1800 pottery, Doulton figures and character jugs of a short production run, would all have shown a considerable profit.

One danger is that when things become collectable, someone produces reproductions and fakes. These should not be confused with the real thing, as the fakes strive to look old and do not have the quality of the originals. Novice collectors must be on their guard.

On one of the *Heirloom* programmes I compared two Toby jugs – an eighteenth-century original at several thousand pounds, with a twentieth-century example at a hundred. The former, with lovely soft, translucent colours, developed by the lead in the glaze, was completely different to the latter, which had hard, glassy and lead-free colours. On another programme I showed a fine dish decorated with slip-trailed designs, which dated from about 1700 (worth £1,000 today) and contrasted it with a similar piece made just a year ago by a modern craftsman potter, that you can acquire for the considerably smaller sum of £20 to £30.

In short be wary of pieces that seem too cheap, or heavy mass-produced pieces that try to look like their lighter, lovingly made originals. To get the feel of the genuine piece, handle as many items as you can.

A group of Doulton saltglaze stoneware pieces with hand-incised scenes of animals, made in Lambeth by Hannah Barlow in the second half of the nineteenth century. Hannah's mark of H and BB conjoined under the base is a guarantee of superb studies of animals and yet the quality does not seem to be reflected in the relatively low prices of her work. Worth about £250-500.

WHAT TO LOOK OUT FOR

Anything you buy yourself should be bought because you love the piece and want to enjoy it. Whether it is an attractive but cracked pot bought for 10p from a box outside a junk shop or a piece that cost you so much money from an antique dealer or auction house that you dare not tell your wife or husband, buy it if you love it and you will never regret it. I only have to write these words to remember a hundred pots that I should have bought but let the opportunity pass by, perhaps because I thought them too expensive or I would get a better one later.

While money should not be the reason for buying a piece, it is still comforting to know that your collection is bought at a sensible price and would lead to a profit if sold. It is fair to say that a good collection of pottery and porcelain bought at a right price will generally hold its own with any other form of investment. As an extreme example I can tell you about a Staffordshire pew

Examples of fine hand-painted fruit studies by Royal Worcester artists. The square dishes and 22cm (9in) dessert plate were painted by Frank Roberts in 1913 as part of a dessert service, the

additional larger 23cm (10in) plates and the oval dish were added to the service in 1922 and painted by Tom Lockyer, as Roberts had died in 1919. The whole service, sold at Bonham's in 1988 for £7,500, is typical of the traditional quality of the fine fruit painting at Royal Worcester.

group in saltglaze stoneware depicting two musicians on a pew bench, made in about 1730. This had been bought for £1 in a Nottingham street market some 25 years ago, the price went up as it changed hands until it was acquired by a collector for £50. It remained in his collection until he died, when it was sold at Sotheby's in 1986 for £102,000, a world's record price for English ceramics.

Not everything will escalate in value like that, of course. Some pieces bought at the height of a craze may go down in value, like stocks and shares. This has happened this year to several types of English ceramics, such as the work of the 'Staffordshire ladies' – designers and decorators of the Art Deco period such as Clarice Cliff and Susie Cooper – which was keenly sought following an ITV series about them. Now the only examples that are sought after are the more exotic versions of 'Bizarre' patterns of Clarice Cliff. Some of the horrendous prices paid for the rarer Doulton character jugs and figures are now more realistic and lest you think that only recent pieces have gone down in value some eighteenth- and nineteenth-century pottery and porcelain has done the same. This is not to say that such pieces were poor or bad investments, but they reflect the changes of fashion and taste of collecting – next year they may go up again. But remember, if you bought the item because you loved it, then such changes of fashion do not matter.

You should also go for quality when buying a piece of porcelain. I think it is better to buy one superb hand-painted plate by a great porcelain artist, than four dozen lithographic printed plates, and likewise one finely gilded vase or cup and saucer than a hundred Japanese eggshell teasets of the 1920s. It is all a question of personal taste, of course; beauty is in the eye of the beholder.

If you are buying with the idea of investment, then you should buy the very best quality and condition piece that you can afford. It is an axiom that a perfect piece is usually instantly saleable whereas a damaged one is difficult. This particularly applies to eighteenth-century porcelain where a tiny chip or crack, or even a little rubbing of the gold, can by frowned on. Slight damage is not so worrying in the case of pottery where because of the more fragile material, you almost expect a little damage. The novice collector should beware of repairs and restoration, which if done recently by one of the many superb modern restorers can be very hard to tell. It is all very well buying a piece that you know is damaged or repaired, but when you find out later that the vase you thought was pristine had been broken off at the foot, the figure's head had been chipped or the plate has a bad crack which has been sprayed over with a varnish, you are bound to feel cross.

A beautiful garniture of three Worcester vases with twisted snake handles and applied 'pearls', and finely painted panels of English landscapes, of the Flight Barr and Barr period, *circa* 1810. This sold for £1,600 in Phillips in 1981, but with the great interest in such fine quality porcelain since then the present day value is likely to be three or four times higher.

15

You can spot repaired breaks in translucent plates by holding them up to a strong light, and feel changes in the surface with your fingers. Suspect any tacky places, which may indicate spray varnish and look especially carefully at danger spots on figures, such as the heads, arms and any projections. Provided no one is watching, you could use a pin to probe a suspect place (a pin will slide off real glaze but jab into a repair). Aficionados can be seen tapping danger spots with their teeth, which are sensitive enough to feel a change in material.

However, do not be put off by damage if you like the piece and especially if it is rare. You can always hope to trade up when a piece in better condition comes along. Although I have said that damaged porcelain should be thought about carefully, there is no doubt that perfect pieces of porcelain are becoming rarer and one day the source may dry up entirely. A great collection of English blue and white porcelain, every piece of which was rare but damaged, was sold at auction a few years ago and fetched over £50,000. The collector, a great friend of mine, had formed the collection over many years, buying rare pieces quite cheaply in such markets as the Portobello Road in London. So you do not need to pay through the nose for a collection, especially if you go against the trend and collect something that is not yet fashionable.

If you are not confident in telling the good from the bad then you should seek the advice of a good specialist antique dealer, who will guarantee anything that he sells. Never be afraid to ask questions; a good dealer will always be willing to help and to give a receipt setting out condition and a description of the piece. Many auctioneers, too, are ready to comment on the condition of a piece.

WHERE TO BUY

There are many places where you can find antique pottery and porcelain, the most obvious being auctions. Do not be frightened to attend auctions, especially on the viewing days when you can handle the pieces, which is a great education in itself. Many auctioneers give price estimates in the catalogue, or will tell you them if asked. Price estimates, however, even by an experienced cataloguer, can vary from the knock-down price. Perhaps because of lack of interest, a lot can go for very much less than the estimate; but if there are two or more people determined to get a particular vase or plate then the price may be sky high. Never be afraid to go and bid yourself for something you like, but set yourself a limit in advance, as the excitement of the moment can cause you to get carried away. If you cannot attend the auction, or if you are shy about bidding, the auctioneer or the saleroom porter will bid for you.

Antique fairs offer other sources for finding antique porcelain and pottery. There are some specialised ceramic fairs, where specialist dealers deal only in pottery, porcelain and glass. The finest of these are vetted, a process in which experts check the accuracy of description and condition and some of them have date lines, in which nothing made later than the published date is allowed to be shown. I often feel it is sad to fix an arbitrary date limit: to suggest that anything made before, say, 1900 is fine but afterwards, beyond the pale. That rules out so many very fine things, even things being made today, which will be the heirlooms of the future.

Another source for finds are Sunday morning car-boot fairs, street markets, and even jumble sales; but be prepared to sift through acres of junk in the hope of finding one really nice piece. Perseverance pays off – do not be deterred by ten visits with nothing to show because the next time something wonderful may be waiting for you. You may not know what the item is or from which factory it hails, but if it speaks to you, grab it! You can have a lot of fun and gain a lot of knowledge in tracking down its origin. If you are buying a piece in such downmarket places, especially for your own pleasure or study, do not worry about the condition. Some of my dearest possessions are wrecks, but what wonderful wrecks!

USEFUL INFORMATION

A large number of books are now available to help those interested in learning more about ceramics. There are even book dealers who specialise in the sale of ceramic books, such as Barry Lamb of 12 Commercial Road, Swanage, Dorset, who will be delighted to send you a catalogue. A number of ceramic study societies exist, putting on regular seminars and lectures and there is sure to be an antiques society near you which you would find of great interest. Of special help is the Antique Collectors' Club of 5 Church Street, Woodbridge, Suffolk who, as well as producing a monthly magazine for members, put on an annual ceramic seminar. One of the main ceramic dealers and authors of this country, Geoffrey Godden of 17-19 Crescent Road, Worthing, Sussex, whose *Encyclopaedia of British Pottery and Porcelain Marks* is the bible in identifying factory marks, also puts on study seminars.

Also look out for the growing number of specialist ceramic societies. A society can develop great interest and knowledge in a subject and such groups as the Friends of Blue (blue printed earthenware) and the Commemorative Collectors' Society (commemorative wares of all sorts) attract growing numbers of collectors.

Late seventeenth-century English delft plate, commemorating the coronation of King William III, with a simple painting in cobalt oxide with touches of yellow. Such examples of this early date are now highly collectable and expensive – this example is worth about £5,000-6,000 – but commemoratives from the end of the nineteenth century onwards may be found at little cost and an interesting collection could be formed.

A FINAL WORD

Here are a few do's and don'ts to remember when you start collecting. Do only buy things that you like and that you can live with. Do discover as much as you can about what interests you; learn the differences in bodies and glazes; try to become expert in your chosen field, which will give you confidence and an edge over other collectors. Do see and handle as much as you can and listen to and learn from experts. Do read as much as possible and remember that good ceramic books can be very profitable things. Do join groups of like-minded collectors and enthusiasts and share your knowledge and love of your collections. However, don't believe everything you are told, especially by the ill-informed. Don't fall for the worst mistakes, such as not spotting repairs and restorations. Don't get caught by modern fakes or reproductions, or think that pieces are older than they are because they are in an old style or have been inherited from someone's granny. Don't believe that all marks are genuine, because many are not, nor think that all good pieces should have factory marks, as many early wares are not marked.

If you can follow this advice, it will lead to happy collecting.

This superb Royal Worcester porcelain model by Doris Lindner of Red Rum, the famous hero of the Grand National, was made in a limited edition of 250 copies. Limited editions are at their lowest point for a long time on the auction market and must represent very good buys if you like and admire the subject, but do go for the highest hand-made quality pieces.

CONTINENTAL PORCELAIN

by John Sandon

Considering the size of the English ceramics industry discussed by my father in the previous chapter, it is surprising that more Continental than English items are brought into an *Heirloom* programme. The vast output of the central European porcelain industry cannot be stressed too strongly, and there is hardly a home in Britain where a Continental figurine is not proudly owned as decoration. The best of these can be very expensive, but many others are definitely affordable and you do not need to be an expert to get a great deal of pleasure from a pretty vase or figure group.

The field of Continental porcelain is dominated by four important names – Dresden (Meissen), Sèvres, Vienna and Capodimonte. Most people have heard of these, and some have even become household names. It may therefore shock many readers when I report that almost every example prized by families under these names is a fake. Maybe 'fake' is too strong a word and I should put it another way. Genuine pieces of Sèvres are very rare, while porcelain was only made at Capodimonte for sixteen years in the middle of the eighteenth century. These names, however, are widely used today for a style of porcelain similar to the original wares.

The products of the great eighteenth-century makers became legendary. One hundred years later there was a considerable demand for copies of the earlier styles, and, while Meissen and Sèvres were still major producers in the nineteenth century, these two factories could not possibly make enough to satisfy the demand. Many smaller makers produced wares in the distinctive styles of the earlier factories, not usually as fakes but as reproductions. These frequently bore copies of the original marks, as no laws prevented such imitation. Indeed, the copies were marketed under the generic names 'Dresden', 'Sèvres' and 'Capodimonte', names still used today.

The names have therefore become almost meaningless. Serious collectors pay considerable sums for rare eighteenth-century wares. At the same time some established dealers and smaller auction rooms sell decorative nineteenth-century vases as 'Sèvres', believing this is the correct name to use. Novice collectors who buy such pieces because they are so colourful and impressive, become concerned when an expert condemns their often expensive purchases as fakes. If you have inherited an heirloom, which for more than a hundred years your family has believed to be fine Vienna, it is hard to accept that it is probably a copy, with an imitation 'beehive' mark. You will naturally be anxious and ask the same expert how you can tell the genuine porcelain from the fake, and he would find it very difficult to explain. It does take a lot of experience, and my view is that it really doesn't matter very much. The name is not what you should be buying or valuing. You can call anything by a good name but, unless the quality matches, the name is worthless.

Large numbers of porcelain pipe bowls were made in Germany and an interesting collection can be formed. These are finely painted examples costing up to £400, while cheaper printed pipes can be found for as little as £20.

BRIEF HISTORY OF CONTINENTAL PORCELAIN

A brief history lesson will help to explain why the name is not all-important. European porcelain started in France early in the eighteenth century with the production of a material known as 'soft paste', somewhat similar to that made in England 50 years later. The main aim of the factories was to imitate the fine porcelain of the Orient, although gradually new and original European styles, more suited to the softer, creamy appearance of the French porcelain, developed. Meanwhile in Germany, at the town of Meissen, the King of Saxony established a factory which by 1720 was producing a much finer, whiter porcelain known as 'hard paste'. Under the control of the King, Augustus the Strong, the Meissen factory produced what is arguably the finest porcelain ever made, proudly marked with the crossed swords of Saxony, or AR, the cypher of Augustus Rex the King.

Royal patronage was very important, enabling Meissen to maintain the highest standards, and in France the Royal Court under Madame de Pompadour gave similar support for a factory near the palace at Vincennes, moving to Sèvres in the 1750s. Financed and protected by the Queen, the Sèvres factory produced the finest quality money could buy, on the soft paste French porcelain which was more suited to delicate rococo styles and scrolling shapes, dominated by richly enamelled background colours.

Let us now jump a hundred years to the mid-nineteenth century. Porcelain was still being made at Meissen, Sèvres and Vienna, both in modern styles and copying earlier wares. Collectors, especially among the English gentry, paid vast sums for the rarest early examples and, needless to say, lots of fakes were produced copying the established styles. Today these fakes are themselves antique, and the considerable confusion exists with which I began this chapter. To help you to understand the situation further, I will discuss the principal makers and styles individually and try to explain what you should be looking for.

Dresden: The Meissen factory was near the town of Dresden and early collectors used the term 'Dresden China' for the products of Meissen. In Dresden in the nineteenth century were established numerous small porcelain makers, in particular decorators who bought white porcelain and painted it in earlier Meissen style. Some of these pieces were marked with the name Dresden, or else copies of Meissen's crossed swords mark. The best known Dresden decorator, Helena Wolfsohn, used as her mark the AR which had been

The AR mark occurs on this 'Augustus Rex' cabaret painted in the Helena Wolfsohn workshop in Dresden in about 1860. Good decoration and worth around £1,000.

used at Meissen more than a century before, and her colourful vases and cups and saucers are known as 'Augustus Rex' ware today. These are now antique themselves and prized by many families because they are so decorative. They are well worth collecting at up to £100 for good cups and saucers or £400 or more for pairs of vases, but do not be misled by the marks, which were used to deceive the Victorians.

Carl Thieme produced some amazing large vases in their factory at Potschappel. Standing 92cm (2ft 3in) high overall, this pair sold in November 1988 for £3,630, a good price, but no factory could manufacture them for that price today.

◇ CONTINENTAL PORCELAIN ◇

The term 'Dresden' is used for virtually all German porcelain in the Meissen style, especially figurines with applied lace trimmings, and ornaments bedecked with cupids and modelled china flowers. The largest factories were elsewhere in Germany. The firms of Voigt at Sitzendorf, Schierholz at Plaue-on-Havel and Carl Thieme at Potschappel between them accounted for a vast output of decorative 'Dresden' china, much of it of good quality. Look out for their marks, all copying Meissen to some extent.

Left A 'Dresden' figure group wearing eighteenth-century costume but otherwise purely Victorian, worth between £500-600. Pretty groups such as this can involve a great deal of workmanship, which is rarely appreciated.

Schierholz, Plaue-on-Havel

Voigt, Sitzendorf

Carl Thieme, Potschappel

Illustrated above, 'Dresden' marks from the three largest producing factories.

The quality of these three factories will not be as high as Meissen, but to most people's eyes just as decorative at a much more affordable price. Meissen itself has maintained the highest quality right up to the present day. Some modern pieces can be jolly good value, especially if you are fortunate enough to find them 'second-hand'.

Vienna: Established in the 1720s, the Austrian state factory reached its heyday at the beginning of the nineteenth century. The speciality was fine quality painting framed in raised, tooled gold on brightly coloured background panels. Scenes were mostly from Greek and Roman mythology. All pieces were marked in blue with a simple shield with two bars which, when viewed upside-down, resembled a beehive. The term 'beehive mark' is frequently used, although this is not really correct. This is probably the most copied of all Continental porcelain marks. Once again the style became legendary, and a great many decorators imitated it, using a copy of the shield mark. The white porcelain plates, cups or vases which the decorators used often already had a maker's mark on them. Look out for the tell-tale sign of a heavy gold rose or green apple painted to obliterate the genuine mark, which is replaced by a copy of the Vienna shield alongside. The situation was further complicated when, on the closure of the factory in 1864, a vast amount of genuine white Vienna porcelain was sold off to independent decorators.

It is therefore virtually impossible to trust the Vienna shield mark at all. Much more important is the quality of the decoration, and a finely painted and gilded copy is just as valuable as a piece from the Vienna factory itself. Look at the piece as decoration, and do not worry if it is Vienna or Vienna-style. Wherever you can afford to, choose fine painting and hand gilding in preference to fine colour printing, a subject discussed in greater detail at the end of this chapter (page 28).

A 'Vienna-style' garniture made in Czechoslovakia early this century with fake beehive marks. Printed gold and photo-litho panels made these cheap, but still highly decorative. They are 37cm (14in) high and sold in 1988 for £270.

Capodimonte: King Charles III of Spain established a factory at Capodimonte near Naples in 1743, and very beautiful figure groups and fine painted services were made there only until 1759. In the middle of the nineteenth century porcelain collectors became confused. They bought other Italian porcelain from the Doccia factory near Florence and the Royal Factory at Naples in the late eighteenth century, and believed these wares had been made at Capodimonte. The Victorian reproductions were marked with copies of the Naples sign of an 'N' below a crown, and were sold as copies of Capodimonte. The style became very popular and was made all over Europe, particularly by the Herend factory in Hungary and by several German makers. Decorative cups and saucers, boxes and caskets were embossed with mythological figures picked out in bright colours, and these are now called 'Capodimonte' by collectors, even though none of them was ever made by the original factory of that name. I prefer to use the term 'Naples-style' for anything marked with the crowned 'N' and once again, the important thing to look for is quality. Some can be very finely modelled indeed, while others, especially those pieces mass-produced in Italy today in a crude pottery, are quite appalling. Since the 1950s a popular range of Italian figurines of children and tramps on benches have been marketed under the name 'Capodimonte'. For the same reason, this name is again meaningless and these pieces should be bought because you like them and appreciate the workmanship, rather than because they represent a long-established Italian tradition.

A casket known as 'Capodimonte' although probably made in Germany in the late nineteenth century. Good examples such as this are worth around £350, although many are far inferior in quality.

Sèvres: The 'soft paste' porcelain made at Sèvres before the French Revolution can be incredibly beautiful. The combination of richly coloured flowers, fruit or landscapes reserved on grounds of deep turquoise, pink or blue, produced a style which is timeless and just as popular today as when Louis XV gave services as diplomatic gifts to the rulers and courts of Europe. In the eighteenth century all pieces were marked with the initial L for Louis XV or XVI, painted as a mirrored cypher and containing a date code letter of either a single or a double letter for each year between 1753 and 1793. This painted mark was never again used by the Sèvres factory.

During the nineteenth and twentieth centuries numerous copies of the prized early Sèvres porcelain were made, all with copies of the original factory mark together with date letters. The most common fake date letter is the first letter of all, A, which should be 1753 but hardly ever is. Many of these Sèvres-style wares were further ornamented with richly gilded mounts and they can look very splendid as decoration in a Victorian or modern home. The best nineteenth-century 'Sèvres' pieces, enriched with raised enamel jewels, are just as fine in quality as those from the eighteenth century, but, while expensive themselves, are worth a great deal less. Considerable experience is needed to tell genuine Sèvres from fake, and in all cases an expert should be consulted. It is worth remembering, though, that even if a Sèvres vase is a nineteenth-century copy, if it is of good quality it will still be valuable and every bit an heirloom in its own way.

After the Revolution many thousands of pieces of white Sèvres porcelain were sold off to china dealers and were later decorated in earlier style. Also in the nineteenth century some pieces of early Sèvres with only simple decoration were 'doctored' with the addition of much more valuable coloured grounds. The cleverest of these re-decorated fakes can fool even the most experienced specialists.

ADVICE ON BUYING CONTINENTAL PORCELAIN

By explaining many of the pitfalls I may have frightened some readers from ever buying a piece of porcelain again. This is certainly not my intention and to make amends let me offer some straightforward advice. Most of the helpful tips given by my father in the previous chapter apply just as much to Continental porcelain. As long as you buy from a reputable dealer or auction room you won't go too far wrong. Just remember that by calling a vase nineteenth-century 'Sèvres' or 'Capodimonte', a dealer is not necessarily trying to mislead you. He is using the name generically. You now know that technically he is wrong to say that his vase is Vienna just because it has a 'beehive' mark. What matters much more is how much you like the piece and whether it is good quality. I will conclude this chapter by illustrating two extremes that represent the differences in quality which you should be looking for.

A range of 'bisque' figures made cheaply in Germany in the 1890s and often placed under domes to keep them clean. The backs were frequently undecorated to keep costs down. Collections of these figures can be very ornamental and are not expensive.

The photograph shows German figurines which we call 'bisque', a name given to porcelain when it has been left unglazed so that the details of the modelling are not lost. The colouring has been applied directly to the unglazed porcelain body which is matt and dry to the touch. Bisque china figures were produced in vast quantities in Germany and Czechoslovakia from about 1870 until the 1930s. Exported in bulk to England, every home had them because they were cheap and cheerful – undercutting the more expensive Dresden and Meissen figures – and providing good decoration at a price ordinary people could afford. Many people who write in to *Heirloom* have bisque figurines, the most elaborate preserved under glass domes to keep them clean and protected. They were made down to a price, cast from a minimum number of moulds, usually hollow and light in weight. Because you do not normally see the reverse of a figure when it is displayed on a shelf or mantelpiece, for example, the backs were left plain, resulting in the nickname 'flatbacks'. Much higher quality Meissen figures, such as the shepherd illustrated, will have modelling all round.

In my view these figures are all undervalued. The Meissen shepherd made in 1750 is worth about £900, a fair sum of money, but if you compare that with £500 for a similar-sized nineteenth-century Meissen figure the eighteenth-century example must be cheap. Rare early Meissen porcelain is very costly, but some pretty shepherdesses and gallants and ladies can be quite reasonable if you are prepared to look around.

On a more limited budget, German bisque figures can be found at very little cost. Because everyone's grandparents had them they were regarded as cheap and commonplace, which indeed they were, and during the 1930s and especially in the 1950s they went out of fashion. Many were condemned to attics where they remain, often well preserved. Search your own attics and cupboards for these figures, and try to buy those which have survived with only minimal damage. They are not great works of art, but the same pleasure they gave their original owners can be enjoyed today. Prices range from about £20 to £100 for a really nice example. Most were originally issued as pairs and a matching pair is worth roughly three times the price of a single figure.

A mid-eighteenth century Meissen figure of a shepherd, strongly modelled and coloured. Sold in 1985 for £900 and worth little more today. Early Meissen figures are now undervalued compared with later examples.

I remember watching an *Heirloom* programme last year when a colourful plate decorated with fruit was shown. On the television screen it looked like finely painted Worcester until John Bly turned it round and it had 'Made in Bohemia' stamped on the back. He compared it with the Worcester original, finely hand-painted and worth about £400. The German copy was decorated by means of a photographic litho print and, while at first sight very similar, valued at only £25.

The technique of photo-litho printing has revolutionised the decoration of porcelain. From about 1880 it was possible to reproduce a design in colours on to porcelain so that it looked hand-painted at a fraction of the cost. The colouring is broken up into tiny dots rather like a photograph in a magazine, and it is necessary to look very closely with the help of a magnifying glass to see that instead of brush-strokes the 'painting' is made up of tiny dots. Frequently these litho prints are signed as if they were by a named artist, but the signature is also printed. On pieces in Vienna-style the name Angelica Kauffman often appears, but she died in 1807 and never painted on china.

Photo-litho prints should always cost a lot less than fine painting. If you can afford it, try to collect good hand-painting, but if you want overall decoration at a cheaper price, some of the earlier litho prints are good value because they are inexpensive but can still add considerable colour to a room and look splendid in the right setting. The best litho wares of all were made by a firm in Poland who, early this century, used the mark 'R S Prussia'. These are now highly collected in America, fetching several hundred dollars for a small vase.

A detail of a panel from a Vienna-style dish. Close examination reveals the tiny dots that make up the photo-litho print.

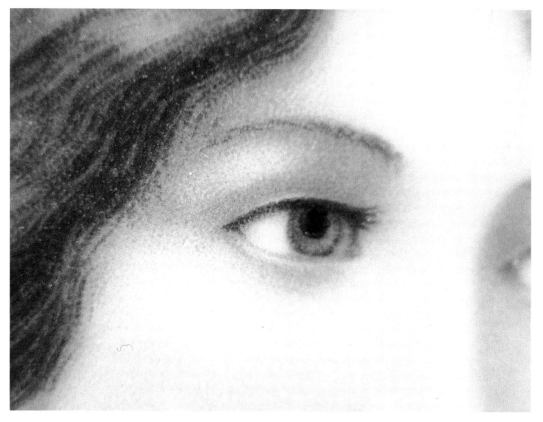

A vase made by the Polish firm of R Suhl bearing the distinctive mark 'R S Prussia'. This is photo-litho printing at its very best. Bought recently in England for £20, the same vase would sell in the United States for around $400.

Finally, the products of a most notorious forger can themselves make a fascinating collection. Samson and Co. of Paris made clever copies of early porcelain such as the vases illustrated here. Their fakes of Chelsea figures marked with a gold anchor still fool a great many people. Don't look on Samson pieces as fakes; instead buy them as quality reproductions with tremendous decorative value and as items to be enjoyed in your home.

Samson of Paris copied every famous porcelain maker. These vases by Samson are 37cm (14in) high and very good value at £700, one-tenth of the cost of an original Worcester pair.

CHINESE PORCELAIN

by Gordon Lang

The truly international appeal of Chinese porcelain is not a new phenomenon. Since the days of Marco Polo late in the thirteenth century it has been admired, wondered at and collected by almost every civilised people. To medieval Europeans, porcelain was an object of great fascination attributed with almost magical properties. This mystery is reflected in some of the early descriptions of the material, such as 'a stone called porcelain' indicating that it was often confused with agate and other semi-precious stones. Porcelain vessels were invariably kept in 'cabinets of curiosities' alongside semi-precious stones, shells and other exotica.

In Europe in the late middle ages, Chinese porcelain would only have been collected by princes and great nobles. By the seventeenth century it had become much more widely available, but still restricted to the wealthier merchant and fashionable classes. Today there is hardly a home in the United Kingdom without a piece of Chinese porcelain. Usually it goes unrecognised as a descendant of those rare early specimens mentioned above.

The vast majority of Chinese porcelain found outside China was made originally for the export market, in contrast to the refined Chinese 'taste' wares for the home market. The epithet 'export', however, does not signify poor-quality porcelain and in many ways it can often prove to be more exciting than the Imperial variety.

Collecting porcelain is a delightful pastime, and, it is to be hoped, a process of acquisition and learning. If one has only limited financial resources it is probably wise to focus on one type or group of wares. This could be blue and white, 'famille-rose', or even monochrome porcelain for the dinner table or display case. Or again one may decide to collect Chinese porcelain vessels based on the forms of European silver wares, or even armorial wares. There are any number of possibilities, all of which will increase your knowledge, thereby giving immense satisfaction over and above the obvious decorative appeal of the porcelain itself.

Within the last 20 years new schools of collectors have tended to avoid cracked or chipped items as in general there is always an 'argument' when disposing of such an investment. Almost every piece of antique furniture, or old painting has been restored yet most people balk at restored porcelain as though it had absolutely no resale value. Demonstrably, this is not the case and a serious collector should always consider rare but damaged items. As I write, a Chinese blue and white pilgrim bottle of the early Ming dynasty with a 'jigsawed' neck has just been sold for £50,000. Not bad for an old wreck!

A Yingqing jar and cover from the thirteenth century. It is carved with lotus under a pale greenish-blue glaze. In the last few years a large number of pieces of Yingqing have appeared on the market, depressing the group value. Although the present object is worth in excess of £10,000, there are many less important looking vessels, especially small bowls belonging to this subtle group, which can be acquired for between £300 and £500.

DEVELOPMENT OF CHINESE PORCELAIN

Porcelain was first produced during the Tang dynasty (618-906 AD). By comparison with today's slick and flawless material, the paste (as the porcelain body is known) was coarse and greyish, rather like dirty chalk. The glaze, too, was relatively primitive, for it was creamy but invariably flawed. But few of us have family heirlooms from this early date. Indeed it is not really until the early seventeenth century that we can expect to find many pieces for inclusion in an *Heirloom* programme. This period is described as 'late Ming', the dynasty which lasted from 1369-1644 AD. A typical example of a piece from this date was the large food jar brought along to the 1988 series. Being of great size, it was made in two parts being joined horizontally two-thirds of the way up. The decoration was of blue on white in rather primitive form. It had been damaged and repaired but still had a value in excess of £4,000!

In order for such wares to be relatively commonplace in Europe today, there must have been significant changes in production and export marketing during the sixteenth and seventeenth centuries. In fact it was the establishment of the London East India Company and its Dutch counterpart in 1600 and 1602 respectively, that signalled the start of the large-scale imports of 'chinaware'.

An early Ming blue and white ewer, dating from the early fifteenth century. The pear-shaped vessel is painted in underglaze blue with a barbed panel enclosing pomegranates, set among trailing flowers. The somewhat blurred appearance of the blue decoration is characteristic of early fifteenth-century blue and white. A piece of such exceptional rarity and quality would realise between £300,000 and £500,000.

For the most part porcelain was considered unimportant, compared with spices, tea or silk, although sufficient quantities of it were shipped to create a 'fashion'. By about 1700 so much porcelain was being imported that there were occasional bouts of indigestion and the supra-cargoes, those responsible for buying such commodities, were advised to buy porcelain only as a ballast cargo.

With the arrival of the Portuguese in Chinese waters during the second decade of the sixteenth century a new chapter began in the history of porcelain. For the first time the potters of Jingdezhen (the main production centre for porcelain) made porcelain to order for Europeans. It was almost exclusively blue and white ware, painted with Portuguese coats-of-arms, inscriptions and even armillary spheres. Such pieces bearing 'foreign' devices must have represented a tiny fraction of the trade for today there are only a few such examples still surviving.

Most of these 'Western barbarian' pieces were rather poorly executed, compared with items made for the Imperial court and the Chinese bureaucracy, which were made to a much higher standard. As the sixteenth century progressed, although there was an overall decline in the quality of the porcelain produced, the gap between Imperial wares at one end of the spectrum and

A blue and white plate, 25cm (10in) in diameter, *circa* 1720-30. The centre is painted with squirrels among fruiting vine, bamboo and aster. The rim is carved with chrysanthemum and peony flowers. The charming subject and the slightly unusual carved border considerably enhance the value of this plate, worth about £300-400. Without the carving, the plate would be worth about one-half or one-third of this estimate.

A blue and white salt from the period of Kangxi (1662-1722). The pan-topped salt reservoir is painted with a Buddhist lion, sometimes called a Dog-of-Fo ('Fo' means Buddha). This salt is based on a European original. Although the salt illustrated is almost 300 years old, one could obtain a comparable piece of this date for between £200 and £300.

export wares at the other, widened, with the export wares being much poorer in quality.

In the last quarter of the century a new style of export porcelain, painted in a rather regimented manner, emerged. The designs on any object, whether bottle, bowl or dish, were broken up into segments or compartments. A typical example would be a dish decorated in the centre with a riverside scene encircled by a border of large and rectilinear panels enclosing conventional flowers and precious (that is Buddhist or Daoist) emblems. This method of composition used a number of fairly simple repeating elements, each painted by a different hand who, after painting his motif, would then pass it on to a fellow worker to add his or her particular motif, and so on until the entire object was decorated. Little skill was required in this method of mass-production, and the factories at Jingdezhen could therefore employ children or labourers under a system of enforced labour.

By the end of the sixteenth century, the Portuguese were shipping huge quantities of this type of porcelain in their enormous ships called 'carracks'. Several carracks were captured by the English and Dutch during the years of confrontation between themselves and their Iberian enemies. Two vessels, the Santa Catarina and the San Yago, were taken by the Dutch in 1602 and 1604 and finally brought to Amsterdam and Middleburg. The cargoes included over

150,000 pieces of porcelain, which were subsequently sold at auction. Among the buyers of this novel ware, called *kraak* (from carrack) by the Dutch, were King James I of England and Henry IV of France. The excitement caused by this exotic porcelain encouraged the Dutch to seek out sources of supply for themselves, rather than rely on foreign entrepreneurs, and it was not long before they had established themselves in the South China Seas using Bantam in Indonesia as their base.

The Dutch influence on the China trade is evident by the 1620s and 1630s from a number of vessels modelled after northern European silver or metal forms: mustard pots, candlesticks, table salts, tankards and ewers, as well as new decorative ware forms, such as the curiously named 'rollwagon' – a tall cylindrical vase with a narrow or waisted neck. Not only were the shapes new but the method of decoration on these pieces of hollow-ware was new, too. Instead of the somewhat mechanical compartmentalised *kraak* porcelain-style which was still to be found on most plates, bowls and dishes, these innovatory European forms were painted to a high standard, either with floral subjects or with narrative themes drawn from Chinese book illustrations. The material of this group appears more refined; the paste, whilst admittedly greyish, has almost no iron-red oxidisation on the margin of the glazed and unglazed area. The glaze is glassier but still of bluish tone, like most Ming porcelain, but is generally freer of the iron spots endemic in the less sophisticated *kraak* porcelains. The cobalt blue is of a purplish hue or, as one authority described it, as resembling 'violets in milk'.

The evermore frequent incursions of the Mongolian Tartars into metropolitan China during the declining years of the Ming dynasty caused great upheaval in the area of Jiangxi where the kilns of Jingdezhen were situated, and by the middle years of the century supplies for the export market were seriously affected, until finally, in 1657, trade ceased altogether. Trade was resumed in the reign of the Emperor Kangxi (1662-1722), but in the interim the Dutch, who by now enjoyed a virtual monopoly of the China trade, had taken steps to obtain porcelain from the Japanese.

The great success of the colourful Japanese Imari wares in Europe during this Chinese hiatus, encouraged the latter to manufacture similar style Imari ware, today not surprisingly called 'Chinese Imari'. Although the colours used are similar – red, blue and gold – Chinese examples tend to be painted in a crisper fashion than their Japanese counterparts.

Following the early troubled years of the Manchu or Qing dynasty (1644-1912) the kilns at Jingdezhen were reorganised and there were a number of innovations, not only in terms of conditions at the kilns (for example the abolition of the system of enforced labour), but also in improvements in the composition of the material, the introduction of new glazes and the revival of techniques that had fallen into disuse.

The porcelain from the reign of Kangxi (1662-1722) is readily identifiable. Most pieces of this period are very neatly potted with a carefully trimmed footring – a pale honey-coloured zone bounding the edge of the glaze on the foot – revealing a pure white paste with just the merest suggestion of iron being present. The glassy glaze is very economically applied, with no streaks or ripples, and the result is a brilliant white porcelain in contrast to the slightly duller and bluish appearance of Ming porcelain. The cobalt blue of this reign is

generally clear and looks more sharply focused, as would be natural under a fairly thin glaze. The painting decorating pieces from this period tends to be repetitive and executed in a conventional manner, and the range of subjects limited. Popular narrative themes are dotted with wooden-looking officials and puppet-like females with submissive, bowed heads. Nevertheless, the end result is rarely other than charming. In terms of design, a typical feature of porcelain jars produced at this time is that they have a generous bulbous shape.

Towards the turn of the seventeenth century there were continued demands of the Dutch and the English East India Companies, not only for run-of-the-mill porcelains, but also for special orders. The indiscriminate demands of the fashionable for blue and white porcelain during the 'chinamania' of the Restoration gave way to more discerning requests. The somewhat random arrangements of assorted porcelain described by Defoe in his *Tour Through the Whole Island of Britain* gave way to more organised displays, particularly on mantelpieces. Now the Chinese potter could furnish suites of tall, slender porcelain vases, of contrasting but complementary forms, and painted with a

A pair of large blue and white hall jars, approximately 61cm (24in) high, dating from the period of Kangxi (1662-1722). Such large pieces are almost invariably damaged, but the illustrated pair, which are in surprisingly good condition, would fetch around £10,000. Comparable but more battered single jars can be obtained for between £500 and £1,000.

matching pattern. Such groups, termed 'garnitures de cheminée', were usually made up of an odd number of vases, most frequently three but sometimes as many as nine. They were made to adorn the mantelshelf, or 'chimney-tree' as it was sometimes known – a stepped or pyramidal arrangement of shelves above a fireplace – which was fashionable at the end of the seventeenth century. Over the years, countless numbers of these sumptuous baroque garnitures have been split up for one reason or another. It may be through a bequest where everything must be seen to be divided up equally, including the garniture. Or it may be through breakage, or simply that some of the garniture was thought to look better in another room in the house and was never reunited, even when the entire contents were sold off in a house sale. Today, garnitures of just three vases are very rare, larger groups of five or seven surfacing only once in four or five years. As such garnitures are worth considerably more than the sum of the individual parts, it seems important that families should take great care when sorting out bequests and family divisions not to split a garniture unwittingly but to keep it as a group.

In the past 20 years I have come across several examples of garnitures scattered about the house by unwitting owners. In a very recent case I managed to reassemble a brilliant Kangxi garniture dispersed about one of the grandest houses in West Sussex. Split, the garniture was insured for about £2,000, but together, it was worth around £8,000. Even if you possess just one blue and white Chinese vase, it is worth having it checked by an expert, just in case it is part of a garniture.

Two 'blanc-de-chine' vessels, 8-10cm (3-4in) in height, dating from the seventeenth century. One is based on an archaic bronze with three feet. The second is based on a rhinoceros-horn carving, the sides applied with prunus blossom and supported on a pierced base. The vessel on the left would cost around £400-500 but the slightly cracked rhinoceros-horn wine cup could be bought for £40-50. A perfect specimen would be worth about £250-300.

Specially commissioned shapes now included monteiths (for cooling wine glasses), vases based on Venetian glass, trencher salts, beakers, mugs after European stoneware originals and bleeding bowls. In addition, orders were placed for table services decorated with personal coats-of-arms.

Until the reign of Kangxi, almost all the porcelain available in the West was blue and white or blanc-de-chine, so named by French connoisseurs in the nineteenth century. The Chinese developed overglaze enamelling in the fifteenth century but few pieces ever found their way beyond the frontiers of China during the Ming dynasty.

In the last third of the seventeenth century, Chinese potters produced a new lustrous palette whose dominant colour was a rich, translucent green. This group was coined 'famille-verte' by nineteenth-century French connoisseurs, who also invented much of the nomenclature for Chinese porcelain, which has now been adopted throughout the Western world. 'Famille-verte' is the luxuriant offspring of the bold Ming *wucai* ('five-colours') palette. Designs, whether of floral, animal or human subjects, tend to be large in scale relative to the size of dish or vessel on which they appear. 'Famille-verte' was itself superseded by the softer, opaque, pastel enamels of the 'famille-rose' group in about 1720. As the name implies the 'famille-rose' palette includes pink, a colour which is inseparable from the rococo style surfacing in France at about the same time. The works of Watteau, Pater, Boucher and Fragonard are composed of colours exactly matching those on the imported 'famille-rose' porcelains. In contrast with the large-scale, luxuriant 'famille-verte' group, the rose or pink group are painted on a smaller scale, and the subjects treated in a delicate or slighter, more feminine manner.

The lightheartedness and aristocratic playfulness of this period in Europe was very much reflected in contemporary Chinese exportware, which tended to follow the occidental fashion. As well as the conventional porcelains copying silver shapes, often painted with Meissen-style flowers, there were tromp l'oeil objects, such as soup tureens, modelled after Strasbourg faience originals in the forms of a duck, goose, falcon or even a wild boar, or flower-holders made to resemble a piece of furniture. Popular too, were services decorated in 'famille-rose' or 'en grisaille', the latter being a technique in which black enamel is used either alone or with a little extra colour. Here the artist painted his subject, which was invariably based on a European engraving such as 'The Choice of Hercules', 'The Judgment of Paris', or 'Don Quixote', with an extremely fine-haired brush, so that the end result was close to the original print. The heyday of these 'grisaille engraving' porcelains (sometimes referred to as Jesuit Porcelain) was between 1735 and 1755, although there are examples following designs by Bartolozzi done in the 1790s.

Jesuit ware generally refers to those wares painted with Christian religious subjects which began to appear in the early eighteenth century. Some are painted in polychrome enamels but many are painted in black enamel in such a manner so as to resemble a print. The presence of Jesuit priests in China in the early years of the eighteenth century is often given as the reason for the arrival of such wares, which were particularly popular during the second quarter of the century. The most common subjects include the Baptism of Christ, the Nativity, the Resurrection and the Crucifixion.

The general rejection of the asymmetrical and whimsical rococo style of porcelain in favour of the more rational neo-classicism in Europe in the 1760s and 1770s is mirrored in Chinese export porcelain. Perhaps the most obvious change is the replacement of scattered sprays of European flowers for regular linked or continuous festoon and swag borders. On dishes, the central decorative zone is relatively small, surrounded by a large undecorated area which is itself enclosed within the formal floral border. The 'famille-rose' palette of the late eighteenth century is much harsher than the pre-1750 colour scheme.

A decline in demand for Chinese porcelain occurred from about the middle of the eighteenth century, in the face of stiff opposition from the expanding European ceramics industry. Factories such as Meissen in Germany, Vincennes (Sèvres) in France and in England the recently established concerns at Bow, Chelsea, Derby and Worcester, were making more refined and up-to-the-minute products.

By the last decade of the century, the newly developed and extremely cheap earthenwares of Staffordshire, particularly creamware, drove the final nail into the Chinese exportware coffin. Knowing about this competition, the directors of the Honourable East India Company decided not to import any more Chinese porcelain in bulk, whilst *dis*honourably declining to inform their main Chinese supplier of their decision. Meanwhile the latter, to his own financial detriment, continued to stockpile porcelain in anticipation of further orders that never arrived.

Porcelain was still imported by private traders, and although there were demands for armorial ware, the range available was very restricted and repetitive.

A 'famille-rose' armorial plate, 20cm (8in) in diameter, dating from the period of Yongzheng (1723-35). The plate is painted in pastel 'famille-rose' enamels with an English coat-of-arms, encircled by four carefully executed flower sprays. Armorial porcelain has now become the preserve of the collector who would probably part with about £1,000 to £1,500 for it. Damaged armorial porcelain is available at relatively modest prices.

The earliest armorial ware – porcelain bearing coats-of-arms – dates from the first half of the sixteenth century, but armorial porcelain is extremely rare until the eighteenth century, when England became the largest importer, commissioning about 3,000 services. The earliest recorded English armorial porcelain is the blue and white jardinière ordered by Sir Henry Johnson, a Blackwall shipbuilder, in about 1695. Instructions as to how to paint the coat-of-arms were sent out to China, and the only extant example of an original drawing is the celebrated Leake Okeover service dating from about 1743. Occasionally the instructions were misunderstood by the Chinese draughtsmen, who returned the service with the instructions painted on to the service, together with the coat-of-arms!

A good Chinese 'famille-rose' jardinière, nineteenth-century, painted with three circular panels, each with a spray of chrysanthemums, the rest painted with sprays of peony, the top with shaped trellis border. Sold at auction in 1987 for £1,375.

'Canton Mandarin' pattern porcelain was the most common from about 1800, and for most of the nineteenth century. This depicted panels of figure subjects, reserved on a dense ground of scrolling foliage, insects, butterflies and birds. This extremely crowded decoration was painted in the same 'famille-rose' palette, but was now swamped with gilding, a garish contrast to the previous spare, neo-classical style. It seems that virtually every British household possesses at least one item of this type. One very interesting example of this

'Canton Mandarin' pattern was an octagonal garden seat which was shown in an earlier *Heirloom* programme. These garden seats also double up as garden lights for they are barrel shaped with patterns of holes cut in to allow a candle to shine through. One can imagine the totally magic effect of rows of these seats illuminating terraces and steps. A decorative feature common to most is the effect of studs in bands along the edges of panels. These represent the dome-headed nails used on the earliest types which were made of wood and covered with leather.

Canton-style flatwares for the table have a wide concave rim, a feature introduced in about 1795, replacing the previous plain flat rim. Tureens are oval with bulging bombé sides, based on contemporary European forms. Other very common Canton porcelains include: wash-sets with bulbous bottles, surmounted by tall straight necks, wash-basins with flanged rims, circular sponge dishes and covers, chamber pots, and rectangular boxes for brushes and soap; tall Indian club-shaped vases with trumpet necks, flanked by applied animal

A pair of Chinese Canton vases, third quarter of nineteenth century, each gently swelling body painted in 'famille-rose' enamels with alternate panels of figures and birds and flowers below a waisted neck, moulded with gilt chilong and buddhistic lion pups. Height 46 cm (18¼ in). Approximate value £1,000.

handles; and nests of cylindrical boxes and covers. All these Canton wares are heavily-potted and covered in a dull, greyish-white glaze with an exaggerated rippled or 'orange-skin' effect, and can even be identified, after a little practice, with your eyes shut!

The Aesthetic Movement of the 1870s and 1880s brought about a revival of interest in Oriental decorative arts including Chinese and Japanese porcelain. There was great confusion about what was Chinese and what was Japanese, or indeed what was good and what was bad. The Movement is often deemed to have begun with the opening up of Japan in the 1850s, but it is generally forgotten that the leading auction rooms in England and France were flooded with the greatest treasures of Imperial China following the sacking of Yuan-MingYuan, the Summer Palace in 1860. Now with such paradigms of porcelain it was possible, at least for the very discerning, to put the familiar exportwares into perspective. Even so, many authorities up until the 1920s still considered Chinese blue and white ginger jars the very height of good taste, a fact confirmed by the gigantic sums paid for them just after the First World War.

A Ming polychrome 'chicken cup', approximately 7.5cm (3in) in diameter, dating from the Chenghua period (1465-87). Of shallow, rounded form, the exterior is delicately painted in *doucai* (which literally means 'clashing colours'). To many, the jewel-like precision and delicacy of these Imperial *doucai* porcelains represent the peak of ceramic achievement. This tiny piece is, in terms of size and weight, among the most expensive man-made objects in the world at close to £1,000,000.

JAPANESE PORCELAIN

by Gordon Lang

Japanese porcelain does not enjoy the same great genealogy as Chinese porcelain; indeed it is a comparative newcomer. Up until the seventeenth century the ceramic tradition of Japan had not strayed far from its grass roots. Humble pottery and stoneware displayed little evidence of courtly sophistication, relying for its appeal on surface texture or spontaneous painted decoration, usually of a vegetal nature. Yet within the space of 60 or 70 years, whilst still retaining their ancestral wares, the potters of Kyushu Island in Japan developed a remarkable range of porcelain, which acquired almost cult status among the great European collectors of porcelain. The Prince de Condé and Augustus the Strong both possessed large numbers of pieces. The latter, who was the patron of the famous Meissen factory in Saxony, built a Japanese palace to accommodate his vast collection, which included Imari and Kakiemon wares from the kilns of Arita on Kyushu Island.

The United Kingdom and Ireland boast many fine collections of Japanese porcelain dating from this early period. An example is the collection at Burghley House in Lincolnshire, which is unrivalled in that the Japanese porcelain was itemised in 1688 and has remained more or less intact ever since, the earliest extant documentary collection of Japanese porcelain.

In the late seventeenth century and for the first half of the eighteenth century, Japanese porcelain, in particular Kakiemon, supplanted Chinese in the affection of the European connoisseurs. This is underlined by the fact that the leading porcelain manufacturers at Meissen in Germany, Chantilly in France (before the establishment of Vincennes) and Chelsea in England all copied Kakiemon porcelain, whereas they generally shunned the reproduction of the Chinese variety (with the possible exception of the white wares of Dehua, so-called 'blanc-de-chine'). In England, for example, the less fashionable manufacturers of pottery and porcelain, such as Lowestoft, Liverpool and Bristol, continued with the now déclassé Chinese porcelains as their source of inspiration.

Japanese porcelain presents more subtle problems to the aspiring collector than does Chinese. There are, for example, fewer obvious categories to contend with – no armorial wares within one's means, virtually no monochromes, hardly any narrative figure subjects, and fewer instances of porcelain based on foreign shapes.

There are two basic types of Japanese porcelain: Imari and Kakiemon. The Imari wares comprise an amorphous group, painted in broad-washed colours and covering the surface completely with designs taken from contemporary textiles. Such pieces were doubtless intended as decorative, eye-catching displays but not for the finely-tuned connoisseur or the collector accustomed to the miniature details of, say, early Meissen. On the other hand, Kakiemon porcelain has a directly contrasting appeal to that of Imari. The very spare and asymmetrical designs emphasise the milk-white porcelain of the former which compels one to handle and admire it as many do, and pay high prices to acquire it.

In my view, the most interesting Japanese porcelains were produced in the second half of the seventeenth century. Whether sophisticated Japanese taste wares or simply cursorily painted pastiches of late Ming porcelain, they all possess great charm. Whilst the Kakiemon wares of this period are expensive, even if damaged, blue and white specimens with chips or cracks can be obtained for as little as £100-300 per piece. It is well worth considering damaged Arita porcelain of this period simply because it is rarer than its Chinese counterparts but will, within a generation, become almost unobtainable as new collectors, especially those from Japan itself, move into this sphere.

Japanese porcelain produced between the mid-eighteenth and the mid-nineteenth centuries, when trade was extremely restricted, is very difficult to date precisely. In fact the lack of any innovation characterises the major

An Arita box and cover (left), 15cm (6in) high, dating from the late seventeenth or early eighteenth century. This unusual box would probably realise somewhere around £1,500 to £2,000 at auction.
An Arita blue and white ewer or teapot (right), 7.5cm (3in) in height, *circa* 1660-80. The rather disorganised design and the collar of strange petal motifs which encompasses the neck, are typical of late Ming. This charming piece is in perfect condition and would cost around £2,000.

proportion of the output. The designs on almost all Arita porcelain tend to be debased versions of earlier ware. The exceptions are the delightful Hirado porcelains, painted with playing children or romantic island landscapes.

Almost all the production in the nineteenth century was geared to the manufacture of vases, bottles, bowls and dishes, decorated in an increasingly mechanical way with greater use of stencils. Attempting to classify such repetitious fare into the neat homogeneous categories of the early period would prove impossible. One should simply buy them by the inch!

It would be reasonable to assume that early Japanese porcelain is hardly the field from which a harvest of heirlooms might be picked. Up to a point this is true, but do not forget that an enormous number of early collections were split up during the last 200 years, resulting in the occasional find of a rare piece in a cottage kitchen.

One such piece came into an *Heirloom* programme two years ago. It was a large late seventeenth-century jar which had been bought in one of those idyllic country cottage clearance auctions back in the 1930s for a few shillings. The owner was agreeably surprised to learn of its 300-year-old ancestry and its value of well over £2,000 despite its damage – in contrast to the work of its Victorian counterpart which would have been in the region of a mere £200 in the same condition!

Compared with Chinese or European porcelains, later Japanese porcelain provides the novice collector with fewer categories on which to focus. Whilst many of the designs on wares are adventurous, unusual or futuristic, most are stylistic adaptations of floral subjects. There are animal and figure subjects on dishes and bowls but they represent only a small fraction of the output. There are figures of Buddhist lions but other animals are very scarce. Humans are rarely vernacular such as one might find in Japanese ivory. The repertoire of figures is almost exclusively of sages or immortals, such as Kwannon (the Japanese version of Guan-yin, the Buddhist goddess of Mercy), Daruma, Yebisu or Daikoku, few of which would have much appeal for the Western collector, unlike the range of figurines produced by Meissen, for example.

Realistically, the collecting of Japanese porcelain has to be confined to wares, assuming for a moment that we are avoiding the colourful but somewhat anonymous Imari porcelains as simply fulfilling a minor role in the interior decorative scheme. In my view it is probably more satisfying to focus on the rarer porcelains such as Hirado or Nabeshima type. The former are mostly small scale, painted in underglaze cobalt blue with delightful landscapes or figure subjects. Nabeshima designs, on the other hand, are invariably vegetal or complex geometric patterns, never figure or landscape themes. The formation of a collection composed of these more unusual later Japanese porcelains would doubtless prove to be a rewarding task, particularly as these wares are relatively cheap compared with the obviously decorative Imari and Arita types.

THE EARLY ARITA WARES FROM 1650 TO 1750

Because of the war in China between the Mongolian Tartars and the armies of the tottering Ming dynasty in the mid-seventeenth century, the kilns of Jingdezhen were unable to supply porcelain for export (see page 36). The Dutch, who were the largest importers of the material, resorted to the infant Japanese industry based at Arita on the island of Kyushu. By comparison with Jingdezhen, Arita was minute, the population being no more than a few thousand as opposed to one million souls (1700). Kilns were limited in number to about 150 (to prevent deforestation); Jingdezhen at the end of the seventeenth century had around 3,000. The first orders were placed in 1657 for some '145 pieces which are various coarse dishes'; oddly enough these were destined for Britain, not Holland. In 1659 the scale of the operation was much greater, for in that year the East India Office in Mocha (Arabia) placed an order for 56,700 pieces of blue and white, mainly coffee cups. From 1657 until the kilns of Jingdezhen were again functioning normally, presumably by 1683, the Japanese enjoyed a monopoly in the porcelain trade.

Many early Arita wares were copies of Chinese dishes. From about 1580 until the middle of the seventeenth century Chinese dishes were shipped in huge quantities to South-east Asia, India, Persia, Portugal and Holland. Potters in the latter three countries made copies of these immensely popular dishes, and so when the Japanese made their versions they were simply following a well-trodden path. The copies were not exact and lacked detail, and the designs became stylised and garbled over the years. But the most obvious difference between these and the originals was the rather robust quality of the material itself. Another characteristic of Arita exportware is the rather softer or blurred effect of the underglaze decoration.

European vessels were used increasingly as models for the Japanese potters in the second half of the seventeenth century. For example, jugs were made like the German stoneware and called *kugelbauchkrug* (literally meaning a 'fat-bellied jug'); likewise the *birnkrug* (a pear-shaped jug) was made, together with salts, apothecary's bottles, bleeding bowls, coffee pots and mustard pots. Almost all the foregoing were painted with designs borrowed from the Chinese, but often with some indigenous elements such as a dense, knobbly scroll.

Left An Arita blue and white dish, 56cm (22in) in diameter, *circa* 1660-80. This plate is a copy of a Chinese *kraakporselein* dish from the late Ming dynasty. In perfect condition this piece should fetch about £1,400-1,800 at auction, but an example of about half the size could be acquired for as little as £200 to £300.

Once the Japanese had mastered the technique of decorating in overglaze enamels, probably in the 1640s, they began producing colourful porcelains for the export market. There are two general classifications – Imari and Kakiemon – although there are many instances where it is difficult to ascribe a piece to either category, as they may possess characteristics common to both groups.

The former type is named after the port of Imari through which much of the porcelain trade passed on its way to the West. No porcelain was actually made there, just as none was made at Nanking in China, although old texts often refer to Nanking blue and white porcelain. Imari wares are characterised by energetic, bold and crowded designs, derived from contemporary Japanese textiles. Most designs are floral with small and large shaped panels of flowering tree peony, blossoming prunus, bamboo and chrysanthemum. The panels themselves are often set on a dense background of scrolling vegetation, resulting in a

Right A pair of Arita blue and white jars, 28cm (11in) high, *circa* 1655-75. A single jar of this very early type and size, in pristine condition, can be obtained for around £1,000 to £1,500. There are, however, many slightly damaged examples which can be obtained for a fraction of this estimate.

Top Left An Arita blue and white ewer, 20cm (8in) high, *circa* 1660-80, modelled in northern European form. This ewer in good condition would cost a buyer about £600 to £800, but a slightly chipped one could be purchased for £200-300.

Top Right A Kakiemon jar, approximately 28cm (11in) high, *circa* 1660-80. The high-shouldered body is painted in typical Kakiemon colours: iron-red, deep sky-blue, turquoise, yellow, black and underglaze blue (for the line borders). Today such pieces are rare, fetching £10,000–£20,000 and, with a cover, as much as £40,000.

Below A pair of Imari jars and covers, 36cm (14in) high, *circa* 1700. Although the illustration shows a pair of vases, it was frequently the case that they would have been part of a larger ensemble or garniture-de-cheminée, comprising three, five or more vessels of different shapes. The present pair would cost between £4,000 and £5,000.

sumptuous decorative banquet. The main palette comprises underglaze blue, overglaze iron-red and gilding, although these colours are frequently accompanied by yellow, manganese-brown, green, black and turquoise. The last two, if used, are applied very frugally.

The second group is called Kakiemon after the potter who, as legend has it,

A Kakiemon dish, 23cm (9in) in diameter, dating from the late seventeenth century. Of decagonal form, it is painted in the typical Kakiemon style and palette with a tiger prowling in a rocky landscape.

was the first Japanese to discover the technique for painting porcelain in overglaze enamels. The name has become synonymous with the sparingly enamelled porcelains which provide a minimalist counterpoint to the dramatic Imari wares. The Kakiemon kilns, however, also produced blue and white porcelains, but all are generally more refined than Imari wares: the potting is neater, the porcelain whiter, the painting more crisply executed, and the great variety of vessels or dishes are mostly small in scale. Designs, which may be floral, animal or human, are arranged asymmetrically – a kind of Japanese rococo. A number of patterns have been given specific European names, such as 'The Hob in the Well', the 'Sir Joshua Reynolds', the 'Lady and the Nightingale' and the 'Flying Fox' (*Der Fliegender hund*). Colours employed include iron-red, deep sky-blue, turquoise, manganese, yellow and black. Gilding is extremely rare.

A regular feature of Kakiemon dishes and bowls is the iron-brown dressing on the rim, a feature which first appeared on Chinese ceramics during the late Ming period around 1630, but which was adopted by the Japanese potter slightly later. Enamelling, that is, overglaze decoration required a further firing

Left A Kakiemon figure of a woman, approximately 33cm (13in) high, dating from the late seventeenth century. The figure shown is wearing loose, flowing robes tied at the waist with a sash. A collector would have to part with around £30,000 or £40,000 for this piece.

Right A large Hododa Satsuma earthenware vase of the Meiji period, from the third quarter of the nineteenth century. This is a good example of a piece of later exportware composed of a close-grained earthenware allowing extremely delicate brushwork never found on porcelain. There is often confusion between Satsuma and Imari. The former, which is an earthenware, has warm, buff-coloured ground with a finely crackled glaze, whereas Imari porcelain has a much colder, white surface.

in the kiln (that is after the decoration and glaze firing). Fewer pieces were treated in this fashion, as it was a difficult process and often resulted in a large number of failures, a fact that was reflected in the selling price of the porcelain at the time.

As well as producing porcelain dishes and bowls, the Arita factories also made models of actors and courtesans, lions, tigers, elephants, turtles, hawks, carp and other creatures. These were either decorated in the Imari or Kakiemon colours of iron-red, turquoise, yellow, black, sky-blue and manganese, or simply left white.

NABESHIMA PORCELAIN
Arita lies in the governorship of Hizen under the dominion of the Nabeshima family, who at some time in the 1660s or 1670s founded their own factory at Okawachi, some 8 miles north of Arita and about the same distance from the port of Imari. From these kilns came the most refined of all Japanese porcelains.

Although the kilns supplied the Nabeshima clan and a number of other aristocratic patrons, no porcelain was sold on the open market. The best wares were made in the first half of the eighteenth century and are virtually flawless, made from the finest clay and covered in a smooth, slightly bluish glaze which is free of any impurities. The great majority of the output would appear to have been dishes of standard sizes, usually round but occasionally octagonal or a more naturalistic form, such as a leaf.

In the eighteenth century the foot was tall in relation to overall diameter, slightly over 1cm (½in) on a dish measuring about 20cm (8in). Decoration was

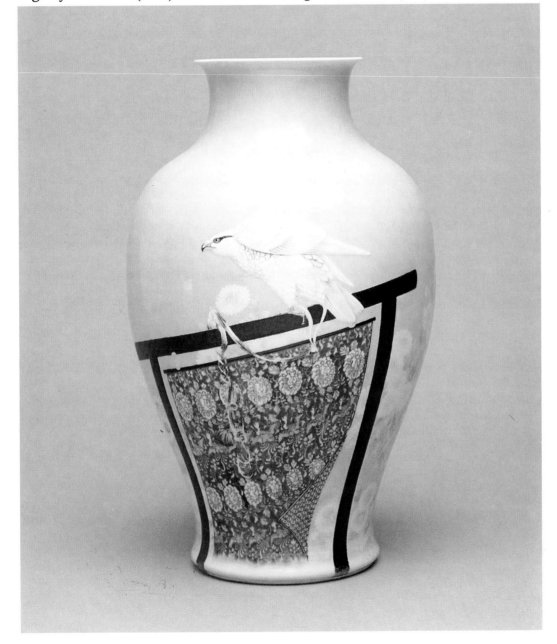

A porcelain vase by Makuzu Kozan, the best porcelain-maker in Japan at the turn of the century, *circa* 1900, 28cm (17in) high. The hawk, much used for sport in Japan, is here in light relief with touches of green and black to the feathers. All birds of prey are good sellers and this vase sold for £9,300 in 1988.

51

mostly a combination of a soft greyish-blue underglaze and clear overglaze enamel colours – yellow, aubergine, red, green and sometimes black. Some pieces are decorated in celadon-green glaze and underglaze blue. Straightforward blue and white is, ironically, quite rare in classical Nabeshima porcelains. Designs tend to be naturalistic, mainly floral, but one also finds trees, shrubs, fruit and birds. Figures, animals or buildings are rarely encountered. The tall foot mentioned above is usually embellished in the most distinctive fashion with a continuous band of underglaze blue teeth termed *kusitakade*, meaning 'comb base'.

DIMINISHING TRADE

The heyday of Japanese export porcelain was the late seventeenth and the first half of the eighteenth century. Then the relative expense of Japanese porcelain compared with the Chinese variety, coupled with a blinkered and inflexible Japanese officialdom, seriously disadvantaged trade. The patience of the sorely-tried Dutch East India Company, which 'enjoyed' the sole European concession for trade in Japan, eventually gave out, and it ceased buying porcelain. Even indirect trade through Chinese merchants dwindled in the second half of the eighteenth century in the face of European competition.

For nearly 100 years from the middle of the eighteenth century, trade in Japanese porcelain was extremely restricted and, partly as a consequence, it is often very difficult to attribute pieces to a narrow date band within this period. The arrival in 1854 of Commodore Perry, an American admiral who opened trade with China, signalled the revival in trade and the beginning of the westernisation of Japan. In the second half of the century the Japanese supplied an eager European market with a variety of goods: furniture, metalwork, ivories and ceramics. The latter category included huge quantities of Kyoto and Satsuma ware, ranging from the most delicately executed miniatures to massive, garishly decorated monstrosities. Neither type can be classified as porcelain, though they are often confused with it.

For the expert, the importance of a thorough knowledge of early Japanese porcelain cannot be overstressed, for the difference between that and its nineteenth-century counterpart can mean, in monetary terms, tens of thousands of pounds. However, the greatest guide for today's collector is the appreciation of quality. After 1856 the range of Japanese porcelain available was enormous, from the very worst mass-produced tea services to the finest vase. Although all of these are 'late' in antique terms their quality rather than age determines their value.

Japanese Works of Art

by David Battie

The choice of title for the series *Heirloom* is an appropriate one. It focuses the mind on the idea that works of art can have a value other than a financial one. In most cases the pieces shown on the programme are appreciated by their owners because they have been handed down the generations, not because they are worth a considerable sum of money. The letters that accompany the photographs sent into the programme reflect this aspect with such phrases as 'I know it's an antique', 'I know it's very old', 'It belonged to my great-great-grandfather', and so on.

In the ceramics field many of the photographs are of Japanese objects. There are several reasons for this, most to do with Britain's position in the world in the last century.

BRIEF HISTORY OF JAPANESE WORKS OF ART

Britain had become a major world power from the time of Elizabeth I and the world leader from the middle of the nineteenth century. We were the explorers, the tea and rubber planters, the traders and the exporters of goods and technical know-how. Wherever we went we bought back souvenirs. We also imported quantities of foreign goods to satisfy demand at home. Coincidentally, with the rise of Britain in world status Japan was 'rediscovered'.

Irritated by troublesome Spanish friars in 1636, Shogun Iemitsu Tokugawa enforced an edict restricting trade to one port, Nagasaki, and to Dutch vessels only. For 250 years the two main islands which made up Japan – Honshu and Kyushu – were *terra incognita* until Commodore Perry of the US Navy sailed into Yokahama harbour in 1853 and announced that the time had come for Japan to open its doors. It did.

Within a few years a major trade developed and by 1867 Japan was able to mount an impressive display of ceramics, bronzes and other works at the Second World Exhibition in Paris. The impact was dramatic: 'japonism' was felt in the Aesthetic Movement, Art Nouveau and in French Impressionism, the latter by accident. From the seventeenth century the Japanese had been devotees of wood-block colour prints, which served much as the political cartoon did in Regency England. It kept a largely illiterate populace in touch with theatrical, literary and social developments. They were unknown to the West and the story goes that Japanese goods arrived in Paris wrapped in prints.

These were circulated round the French artists and print-makers, who found inspiration in the strong structure, bold colouring and flat planes. Amongst the most amusing to our eyes are those that allow us to see ourselves as the Japanese saw us 100 years ago: unrefined, large, hairy and in all probability smelly, as we did not at that time share the Japanese obsession with cleanliness – we were objects of wonder and comment. Nearly a century previously the Dutch had aroused the same interest and were carved as caricature figures (*netsukes*) wearing their outlandish costume. Some of the prints depict the arrival of still greater wonders, such as iron-clad ships and the railway train.

A wood block colour print by Ippousai Yoshifuji of an Englishwoman and her son sightseeing in China. The curious inscription IGIRISWZIN (top right) will, if you try pronouncing it, come out roughly as 'English-woman', the closest phonetically that the Japanese could get. A highly amusing and decorative print which would make about £2,000-2,500.

WHAT TO COLLECT

Japanese prints today can be remarkably expensive if one makes for the rarest of the rare – Sotheby's recently sold an Utamaro for £220,000 but at the other end of the scale many of the nineteenth-century prints can be had for £50-100. One should always try to buy any object in good condition but with prints bought as decoration one might accept a trimmed margin, a small tear or a crease. Many were made as triptychs – three prints in a row forming a single horizontal picture and it is important to avoid buying one part only. Again, buying examples with faded colours or a rubbed surface will probably detract too much from the pleasure of ownership. Pound for pound in colour and impact it would be difficult to match Japanese prints for decoration.

A pair of Imari vases of large size, well painted in bright enamels and gilding with pheasants, *circa* 1900, 105cm (40in) high. Sold for £8,800 at Sotheby's in 1988. They will undoubtedly be sold as decoration, not to a collector of Japanese porcelain.

Japanese porcelain is probably the oldest type of antique we are at all likely to run into. And Arita porcelain is probably the oldest sort. The kilns at Arita had been firing since about 1600 but the blue and white dishes, vases and bottles made in large numbers for the Dutch trade began to flow in the middle of the seventeenth century. Many were made as copies of Chinese blue and white from Jingdezhen but were never a serious rival as they were more expensive than the original.

The so-called Imari porcelain was also made at Arita and exported through the port of Imari from whence it took the name. The characteristic palette of underglaze blue, iron-red and gilding had remained in production almost continuously for 300 years. While the products of the seventeenth and early eighteenth centuries are easily recognisable by the inky blue, heavy potting and grey-blue glaze, we have no sure idea of the chronology of the pieces made from about 1750 to 1850. A few clues are appearing in the clobbered (extra decorated in Europe) pieces in which the style and colours used suggest that much Imari is earlier than we thought. The pieces made from the middle of the nineteenth century through the first 30 years of this vary in quality from appalling to good. Such was the generally poor state of Japanese ceramics in the 1870s that the decision was taken to set up a factory called Fukugawa to set new standards. In this it was successful and pieces with the leaf spray, Mount Fuji or name mark are of fine quality.

Only one major individual porcelain manufacturer is worthy of mention around the turn of the century: Makuzu Kozan. His highly individual potting and decoration stand out from the rest and did so at the time as he was singled out for mention in an article on modern Japanese potters in *Studio* magazine in 1910.

There is one form of porcelain that appears above all others and that is the eggshell tea service. There must have been millions of these produced and most have survived. They are too thin for practical purposes – the tea gets cold the minute it is poured in and they are very fragile. The result is a glut. Worse still they are rarely of good quality – I have only seen a few of any merit in the past 20 years. The result, of course, is a very low market price. Most eggshell tea services to serve 12 people – cups, saucers, plates, teapot, milk jug and sucrier – can be bought for under £60.

An eggshell porcelain plate and milk jug poorly enamelled and gilt with ladies in a garden, *circa* 1920, plate 16.5cm (7in). This is about as bad as these very thin services get and they have unfortunately survived in enormous numbers. £1-10 per piece.

Porcelain that is beginning to attract some attention particularly in the United States is Noritake. It was made for European consumption in the style of contemporary English and Continental factories such as Royal Worcester, Derby and Vienna. The quality is not as good but it is far cheaper. A reasonable pair of vases with flowers on a blue ground are about £80 whereas the same from Worcester would be £700-1,000. Considerable numbers exist showing Egyptian scenes, probably answering demand generated by the discovery of Tutankhamun's tomb. They are less appealing than the floral, and cups and saucers or odd plates start at about £5.

A pair of Kutani vases well enamelled in the typical palette of iron-red, black and gilding with ladies in a garden on one side and birds and flowers on the other, *circa* 1890, 33cm (12in), painted mark Kaga Kutani sei. (Made in Kaga province at Kutani.) £300-500.

The products of Kutani in Kaga province are also not uncommon and are readily identifiable. The porcelain body of the vases, *koro* (incense burners), services and large dishes are decorated with figure subjects, birds and landscapes in iron-red, black and gilding. Most are of good quality, some very good, and the price is dictated by that factor and size.

As with much of the market nowadays, large is beautiful. A pair of Kutani vases 8cm (5in) high could be worth £40 a pair, 16cm (10in) high, £150, but a pair 65cm (24in) high could be worth £800-1,200, the quality remaining the same. Anything that can be made into a lamp base is also much in demand and damage here will matter less as the piece can be drilled to take the flex with no further loss of value. It is also worth noting when thinking of starting a collection that pairs of vases fetch at least three times that of a single.

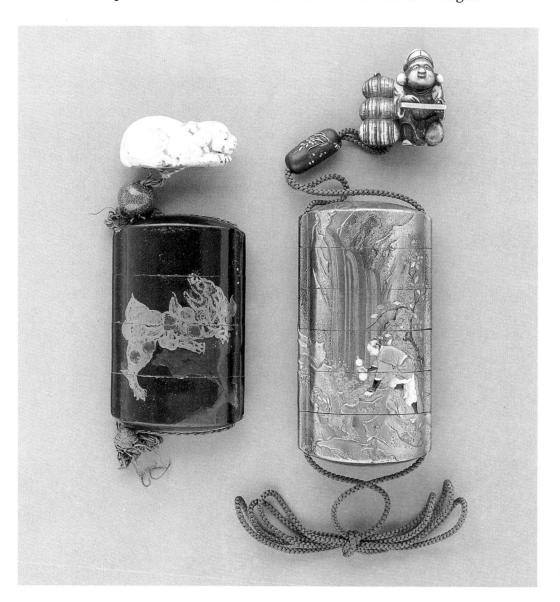

Two lacquer *inro*. *Left*: poor quality, with a gilt *karashishi* or lion dog, mid-nineteenth century, with porcelain netsuke in the form of a sleeping puppy, £70-100. *Right*: fine quality Shibayama style *inro* inlaid in mother-of-pearl and stained ivory with a traveller filling his gourd at a waterfall, *circa* 1900, ivory netsuke of Diakoku, the god of food production, £2,200-2,800.

Lacquer was another Japanese material to have influence in Europe. The technique of lacquering had been learned from China but brought to a perfection in Japan unknown in its birthplace. The material itself has unusual characteristics which make it ideal on which to serve food. It is resistant to heat and alcohol, waterproof, strong and light, and lends itself to decoration. It starts life as the highly poisonous sap from a species of the tree *rhus* but after preparation it is no longer toxic. It is painted in layers on to a body of thin wood or fabric in coats that may be a hundred deep on the best examples. Incorporated into the last translucent layers can be minute flakes or squares of gold leaf to form patterns or shading to a design.

Figures can be inlaid into the lacquer in mother-of-pearl, ivory, coral, tortoiseshell or other materials to build up detailed pictures illustrating Japanese life or mythology. The technique is known as *shibayama* after its earliest exponent.

Furniture is almost non-existent in the traditional Japanese house and boxes, usually lacquered, were used to store everything. After Western trade expanded towards the end of the nineteenth century, the lacquer manufacturers found their highly finished and detailed work in great demand. Screens, boxes, small chests, shelved cabinets known as *shodana* and even the now defunct *inro* (small nest of boxes) were produced for export, the gold lacquer appealing most to foreign eyes. While it cannot be challenged in terms of inventiveness and technical brilliance it has mostly lost the strength, balance and understated beauty of the eighteenth-century and earlier work.

Japanese metalwork was greatly influenced when Japan opened up to the West, and the impact on the commercial and family life of Japan was revolutionary. The samurai had for centuries enjoyed the respect and fear of the general populace and had as its symbol the carrying of two swords: the long sword – the *tachi* – for fighting, and the shorter *tanto* for use as a dagger and disemboweling himself if ordered to do so by his overlord. Apart from the blades there were specialist craftsmen making the elaborate mounts for the scabbard and the *tsuba* or sword guard. *Tsuba* have survived in vast numbers and are seeing something of a flat period in collecting at present. The skill in forging, casting and chasing, of inlay work in gold, silver and other metals is well represented on *tsuba* and a collection could be formed with no great difficulty. Prices range from a few pounds for a rusty iron example 200 years old to several thousand pounds for the best examples.

In 1877 the wearing of swords was banned and the smiths turned to making utilitarian objects introduced from the West and works of art for export. The meticulous gold and silver inlay work of Komai displays the skills learned on sword mounts perfectly. The cast iron body has been patinated and on the best examples where the damp has not rusted it, it is burnished to a dull gleam. The gold is beaten into engraved lines, relieved by *shibuichi* – one of the extraordinary amalgams of metal the Japanese developed, in this case based on silver.

By the end of the century the quality of the metalwork, as in so many other areas, had deteriorated through the insatiable demands of the overseas market. Small objects, particularly cigarette cases, had appeared with a painted black background and flat gilt designs, usually landscapes incorporating the ever-popular Fujiyama. The interior of the case proudly declares: 22K gold. So it

A wonderful quality ivory owl on a tree stump, eating a locust, carved by Ryusai, the eyes inlaid in mother-of-pearl and horn, 11.5cm (4in), *circa* 1900. Owls are very popular subjects whether carved, painted or stuffed. This one would make £1,000- 1,500 despite its small size.

is but there is precious little of it and the 'gold' interior is only plated.

Swords continued to be made in limited numbers mainly for export in over-decorated ivory scabbards and are very poor quality. Gone were the days when a blade could be five years in the forging, although a few were made, mainly as presentation pieces from the Royal Household to visiting dignitaries. Many of the scabbards seen in great numbers in antique shops are not ivory but bone. The two materials can be distinguished from each other. While ivory presents a completely smooth surface, showing striations which appear and disappear when the object is turned on itself, bone has black or brown dots or lines which cannot be carved away.

Japanese sculpture was limited to large figures of Buddha for temple use or minuscule work on *netsuke* (toggles). There are no portrait busts, no memorials, no animals or birds. In this area, too, the West had enormous influence sparked off by the change in dress. Both men and women wore the kimono which had no pockets. Small objects were carried on the person in a small nest of boxes (*inro*) or a pouch hung at the waist from the *netsuke* tucked under the waistband (*obi*). Netsuke literally translated means 'root attachment', which is how it started out life, later to become a major art form. The Western suit was adopted and, as it sported pockets, the netsuke-carvers were rapidly without livelihood. They turned to carving larger groups illustrating Japanese life. There was a ready market for these, both abroad and from the increasing numbers of visitors, including hoards of honeymooners on round-the-world trips.

The carvings grew in size from the tiny netsuke to the massive group illustrated, which is over 60cm (2ft) long. The quality can be breathtaking and compares with the best of European carving of any period. It is also highly prized; the large group fetched £46,000. The value of the carvings demonstrates well, at any scale, the innate skill the Japanese seem to have of miniaturisation and observation.

Ivory was an expensive material and the offcuts from larger sculptures were sold to other makers who used them to form figures or groups. These sectional pieces can be high quality but are more usually very poor. Bone was often substituted for some of the parts to save cost. These less good groups can be bought for about £25, whereas a fine sectional group by Ogawa Seiho can be several thousand. Mass-production to fulfil insatiable demand led to a fall in standards and in 1887 the Tokyo Art School was founded to teach traditional skills. Amongst the first professors were Ishikawa Komei and Yoshida Homei, who carved the large

Left An iron cabinet in the form of a shrine, the doors opening on a series of drawers, inlaid in gold by Komai with dragons and landscapes, late nineteenth century, signed Nihon kuni, Kyoto ju, Komai sei (Made by Komai, living in Kyoto in the country of Japan.) 37cm (14in) high. Sold in 1988 for £13,200.

Below Three netsuke: (*left*) a wood study of a boar well engraved and with a good patina, school of Masanao of Yamada, early nineteenth century, £800-1,000, 3cm (1¾in); (*centre*) ivory boar by Ikko, late eighteenth/early nineteenth century, an attractive carving but slightly disfigured by age cracks, 3.5cm (2⅛in), £1,300-1,500; (*right*) modern plastic reproduction, 3cm (1¾in).

group. The Japanese are at present very selective in which ivory carvings to buy back and want only nobles, samurai or figures from mythology. They don't want peasants.

The Tokyo Art School sculptors also worked in bronze and these too are as good as their European counterparts of the nineteenth century. The animal bronzes of Genrokusai Seiya are powerful studies, well cast and with a fine patina. Most are signed and there is a ready market for them both in Europe and in the United States. Elephants, the most common, can be bought for about £80 for a small example, up to about £2,000. Other, rarer, animals, such as camels, deer or monkeys, can be more expensive. We see all too often bronzes which have mistakenly been polished by their owners. Bronzes have a chemical patination added to their brassy surface at the casting works or by the artist and this rich black/brown colour should not be removed. A damp cloth will remove dust. Inferior 'bronzes' were made using the cheaper, softer pewter-like materials and then patinated. They can be distinguished from real bronze as they dent and scratch easily and the white metal usually shows through on the base.

A rare and massive Tokyo School ivory group by Yoshida Homei, superbly carved with great sensitivity and, despite its size, in good condition with few age cracks. Probably an exhibition piece. *Circa* 1910, 67cm (25⅝in) long. Sold in 1988 for £46,000.

The nineteenth-century earthenware of Japan is one of the most interesting areas and presents a few problems. Much was made at Satsuma in a creamy-coloured body under a clear glaze which breaks into a fine network of crazing. It is then decorated in brilliant enamels and gilding with stylised floral patterns, figure subjects, wildlife (particularly birds) and flowers. Some pieces bear dates usually from the early nineteenth century, but these are now believed to be spurious. Most are signed with the name of the artist and often the Satsuma *mon* or badge, a circle containing a cross. These boldly decorated pieces vary in size from a few centimetres for small dishes and *koro* or incense burners, up to 2 metres. The potting tends to be heavier than the finely decorated pieces but they display a bold strength and typical Japanese skilled handling of the brush and pattern making which makes them splendidly decorative. Their price has risen considerably from the early 1970s with few pieces now fetching under £500.

A Satsuma vase enamelled in sombre tones of brown, black, dull red and gilding with immortals and attendants, *circa* 1890, 16cm (6in), unsigned. Because the design is so flat, muddled and dreary, the vase would only fetch about £70-100.

A fine earthenware plaque by Unzan, enamelled and gilt with figures outside a Shinto temple within an elaborate brocade border, *circa* 1900, 34cm (12⅝in); signed Dai Nihon (Great Japan, Unzan zo, made by Unzan). Sold for £3,300.

Whereas the porcelain was mostly the work of a few large operations, the earthenware makers at Satsuma and Kyoto were much smaller concerns, ranging from one man working on bought-in blanks to perhaps 50 at the larger factories such as Kinkozan's. Sobei Kinkozan is one of the most highly regarded of the turn of the nineteenth, early twentieth-century makers, his work being collected on both sides of the Atlantic. Prices have risen dramatically over the last few years and pieces that fetched £200-300 are now in the region of £1,000.

A fine cloisonné vase and cover by Namikawa Yasuyuki, one of the leading cloisonné makers, using silver wires, *circa* 1900, 8cm (4⅝in); signed on a silver plaque Kyoto Namikawa. Sold for £10,000. The designs for this vase have survived and been published in the *Kyo Shippo Monyo-shu* by Tanko-sha Ltd.

To rival the quality of his work there are two other, smaller, manufacturers: Yabu Meizan and Ryozan, the former producing the more detailed work and stronger demand. The subjects depicted on these later pots are scenes from Japanese domestic life: tea and rice cultivation, festivals, peasants at work, fishermen, mothers with their children, flowers, birds and butterflies, all in the most minute detail.

There were hundreds and hundreds of other makers producing work at this time, ranging in quality from appalling to very fine with a wide range in price. The worst examples in good condition can be bought for as little as £15 whereas the best Yabu Meizan could be £15,000. It is no coincidence that many of the makers' names end in *zan*, the Japanese word for mountain. The Japanese have the curious habit of changing their names during their lifetime as and when whim or circumstance dictates. Apart from their given birth name they may adopt the name of the master under whom they served their apprenticeship, change it again when they start out on their own and several other times for no good reason. This makes tracing their working lives difficult for the researcher. When buying, look for clear, bright enamels and gilding on a clean fine body. The sombre browns and blacks of makers such as Hododa are not desirable. Check thoroughly for condition as the crazed body makes a crack or clean break difficult to spot. On the other hand restoration is difficult to disguise as the fine crazing of the glaze is impossible to reproduce.

Cloisonné was a technique that took Japan by storm at the turn of the century. Originally a European technique that made its way to China and thence to Japan, it was brought to its greatest perfection there. Its production is complex and demands great skill. A copper form such as a vase is beaten from sheet metal and the design drawn on in pencil. Thin wires are then fixed to the body forming small cells which are filled with coloured enamels (glass paste). The pot is then fired, allowed to cool and polished. Different firings are needed to build up the design and different temperatures for the various colours. Some of the polishing on the best pieces was supposed to have taken up to a year. As with so many Japanese works of art there is a whole spectrum of quality to choose from. The poorest examples, many dating from the 1880s, can be bought for £30-50, the best are up to £10,000. The wires forming the design are normally made of copper or brass; on the best they are silver or even gold. A rare technique was to remove the wire barriers with acid to produce a result more akin to a picture. These are known as wireless cloisonné. Cloisonné is impossible to restore satisfactorily and damaged pieces should be avoided.

Japanese works of art of any period are undoubtedly amongst the greatest produced anywhere in the world. For quality, decorative value, inventiveness and sheer technical virtuosity they are unparalleled. We are lucky that in the last hundred years our ancestors were such inveterate travellers and bargain hunters and brought back so much to this country. Much of it is now appearing from attics and cupboards, some to be given its first airing on *Heirloom*.

SILVER & EPNS

by Brand Inglis

The majority of silver and plated items offered for inclusion on the *Heirloom* programme span a period from the 1750s through to the late nineteenth century, from the one extreme of the elegant presentation cup with its intriguing inscription, to the other – the bizarre Victorian centrepiece formed as a desert island complete with palm tree and shipwrecked mariners. It's amazing that on two separate programmes, two items from the eighteenth century referred to the same royal physician in their presentation inscriptions. This is just one aspect of silver heirlooms that makes this study so fascinating, and they don't have to be expensive or valuable to have a story to tell.

STYLES OF SILVER AND EPNS

Before I give suggestions about what you can collect, I feel that I must discuss styles and stylistic change. Although I am no slave to what can best be described as 'period purism' there are, nonetheless, things that do not sit happily together. For instance, many ultra-modern objects go very well with simple seventeenth-century oak furniture and furnishings, but seventeenth-century Spanish brass candlesticks simply do not and can never look anything but outrageous on a Hepplewhite gilded satinwood card table.

Taste and fashion in the decorative arts change, as a rule, from the exuberant to the austere and, though it is always possible to find an object that breaks this mould, it is not a bad rule of thumb. If we start at the Restoration of the Monarchy in 1660, we find the Dutch florid taste prevailing. This is followed by the pure symmetry of the grand Louis XIV style which was introduced to this country largely through the advent of the Huguenots, the persecuted Calvinist Protestants who fled from France in the years around 1685. The native English goldsmiths, generally unable to cope with the high degree of technical prowess needed for the more masterful objects in this great genre perfected a simple style which was in vogue from about 1700 to 1735. At this point, a new explosive force of dynamic design, emanating again from France and known as rococo, reached England. Once again the Huguenot goldsmiths were the more proficient at this superb and complex style which lasted from about 1730 to about 1775.

The Grand Tour excited a reaction against this flamboyant and almost undisciplined style and from about 1760 we begin to see a gradual change

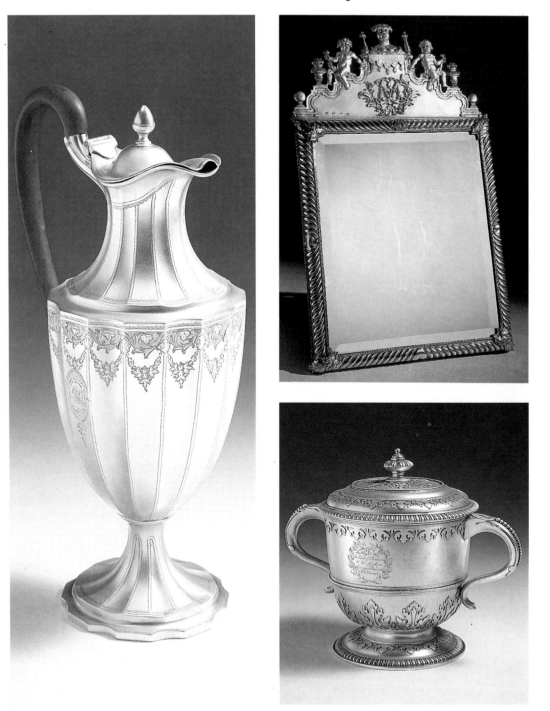

towards the symmetry of the neo-classical style. Though sometimes full of ornamentation, it was strict and refined and frequently quite simple and unadorned. It was followed by a somewhat more grand style of neo-classicism practised by, amongst others, the great English goldsmith, Paul Storr. Though grander and more elaborate than its more delicate predecessor it was still in a

Left A typical survival from the neo-classical period. This jug, with beautifully worked, bright-cut engraving, was made in 1780 and is a most elegant example of the genre. Worth about £2,500-3,000.

Top right A fine William and Mary looking-glass showing the rather flamboyant style still in vogue, though the change to a more severe style was imminent. This was made in London in 1691 and is worth about £15,000-18,000.

Bottom right A beautiful cup and cover of 1692, which shows clearly the new style of ornament and the clean-cut features of the new 'French-inspired' taste. This fine cup was made in 1692, and is worth about £6,000-7,000.

strict neo-classical taste and these periods could be said to dominate the years 1760 to about 1820.

The nineteenth century is rather more difficult to construct in quite such simple forms. The greater use of mechanisation, a vastly growing middle class and a country at the apogee of its greatness gave rise to a shattering amount of cross-fertilised styles and innovative brilliance; it is from about 1820 to about 1900 when it can be argued that we led the world in design and certainly in technology and, though we borrowed ideas from abroad, we no longer slavishly followed fashions and stylistic changes from Europe. This was the case until the end of the century when an amazing revitalisation in France brought the 'Art Nouveau' to an astonished audience. This beautiful creation of fluid movement harks back in some respects to the first rococo movement and inspired a revolution of simplicity known as the Arts and Crafts Movement, which was a turning away from all forms of mechanised art and a return to simple basics. I find that the total lack of any pretensions to sophistication of the Arts and Crafts Movement, though much of it has a simple charm, does not draw me to it, whereas the sinuous beauty of the Art Nouveau I find utterly compelling.

The whole reason for that briefest of introductions on style is perhaps to see more clearly where our own tastes lie and also to judge what can go with what and what cannot.

A Victorian parcel-gilt set of a jug and two beakers made by Messrs Barnard & Co, 1877-8. Quite beautifully made, it shows the Victorian Aesthetic movement at its best. Worth about £2,000-2,500.

WHAT TO COLLECT

One item that everyone seems to have is an old spoon of some sort. Perhaps just one, for jam or sugar, or maybe a complete set for coffee or tea. Whatever the number, age or value, a spoon is among the best possible items with which to start a collection of silver heirlooms for the future. Let us therefore begin with a look at the basis of our table silver: the fork and spoon, known as flatware and the knife, known as cutlery.

Left to right: Dognose tablespoon with rat-tail bowl of 1704; plain rat-tail tablespoon of 1719; three-pronged table fork of 1735; four-pronged Old English pattern dessert fork of 1804; fiddle pattern dessert spoon of 1825; King's pattern teaspoon of 1840.

Silver flatware comes in a number of different styles and the sort that we are familiar with today began to take form in the earliest years of the eighteenth century: the forks had three rounded prongs and the spoons an attractive elongated bowl with roughly parallel sides, and both had a shield-shaped top. This shield-shaped top disappeared fairly quickly and the top took on the simple rounded form that we normally associate with the 'rat-tail' pattern today. On forks and spoons of this period the hallmarks will always be found at the bottom of the stem and, most likely, will be three in number plus a maker's mark, thus four marks in all.

After 1783 the marks were always struck at the top of the handle. Remembering this fact makes it possible to give an 'early or late eighteenth century' dating simply by feeling the marks on a spoon without looking – a trick that will impress your friends no end. After 1784 the addition of a duty mark brought the number of marks up to five, which number remained obligatory until 1891 when it reverted to four.

An interesting set of George IV teaspoons, cast as vine leaves and with bunches of grapes. The same pattern can be found in the mid-eighteenth century but the early nineteenth-century ones tend to be rather better made. Worth about £500-600.

As the century progressed flatware changed, the first most noticeable alteration being that from three to four prongs on the fork, but soon the spoon bowls began to change into more of an egg-shaped design. This was swiftly followed by the ends of the spoons turning down instead of up and the prongs on the forks becoming rectangular in section rather than round. In the nineteenth century a new form came into being, known as fiddle pattern, and then as the century unfolded there came about a great proliferation of patterns, many of which are no longer made today but a good number that are.

As a group, silver flatware represents a vast and interesting area for collecting as it is usually possible, having decided what pattern you like best, to collect in small bits and pieces, thus not straining the wallet too far. As an indication, a full set (60 pieces) of Old English pattern flatware *circa* 1790 will rest in the region of £6,600, whereas individually the pieces may be bought for around £40 each.

Fiddle pattern is a good one to go for if you like a plain and simple design; if you prefer a rather more flamboyant feeling, choose King's pattern. I choose these because they are relatively common and it is not too difficult to find sets of six or even smaller groups to start you going. These patterns were made from the early nineteenth century up to the present day so it gives you a fairly wide choice. Alternatively, if you have some silver or silver plated flatware tucked away, get it out and enjoy it. Give it a good clean and good wash in hot water and liquid soap and then, if you use it every day the act of washing it will keep it clean and you will find it only needs to be properly cleaned once or twice a year at most. If, on the other hand, you are not going to use it all the time (a pity in my view) then it is best to purchase special flatware rolls. These come in a purple-coloured material and have 12 holes which hold up to a dozen spoons, forks or knives in each; this is then rolled up tightly and it keeps the air off the silver so keeping it tarnish-free for months.

These three photographs give an example of the versatility of a pair of candlesticks that can be turned into candelabra. *Top left* Corinthian column-form candlesticks. *Bottom left* Reeded leaf-capped branches with a flame-finial in the centre (or this can be removed to turn them into three-light candelabra), on the original Corinthian column candlesticks. *Right* Finally, the two branches can be put on one candlestick to turn it into a four- or five-light candelabra. All made by William Hutton and Sons, London, in 1899. Worth about £3,000-3,500.

Candlesticks or candelabra are beautiful additions to any table or indeed any room. The difference in price between various sorts, however, can not only be puzzling but downright daunting for the silver-collecting novice, and therefore a short explanation might be helpful and, hopefully, clarify rather than further muddy the waters.

First, it is best to understand that practically all eighteenth-century candlesticks have been reproduced in the nineteenth and twentieth centuries and the price difference between original and reproduction will be substantial. Second, from the last half of the eighteenth century it was possible to die-stamp candlesticks from very thin metal and then fill them with pitch to give them substance. The difference in price between cast candlesticks and filled candlesticks is also substantial, thus there can be a vast array of different prices from a cast early eighteenth-century candlestick to a twentieth-century filled reproduction example.

In addition to this, legions of candlesticks from about 1770 to the present day were made in plated silver, Old Sheffield plate to begin with, then, later, electro-plate. This brings a further price differential into the problem and in the end it is only possible to decide what you want, balanced by what you can afford, by looking at lots of examples. It is also worth having discussions with a good friendly dealer who will try to get for you the best possible selection to suit

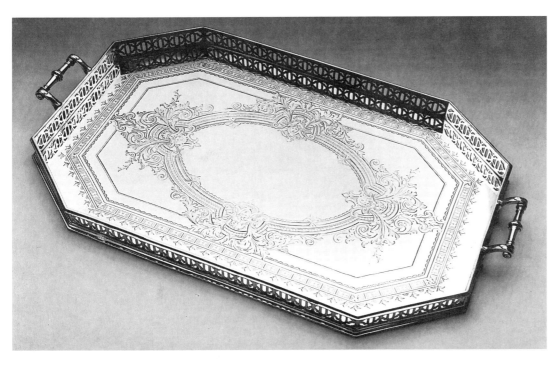

A fine example of a Victorian silver tray made by James Garrard in London, 1883. Worth about £2,500-3,500.

A beautiful set of tea caddies from the rococo period. These were made in 1740 and, though the outline is still plain, the decoration is full of movement and vitality. Note, too, the shell finials. Worth about £8,000-10,000.

your price bracket. By and large, antique dealers are very willing to be genuine friends and counsellors and give you the best possible help and advice after you have told them roughly what it is you are looking for.

Collecting salt cellars, pepper mills and mustard pots might be overdoing the idea of silver on a table, and the whole thing can, if allowed to get out of hand, begin to look more like a pretentious hotel rather than a home so a balance has to be struck. Let us suppose that you now have a full set of silver flatware and four silver candlesticks on your table and that you have a very nice plated basket to use as a centrepiece. That is quite a lot of silver or silver-coloured metal and it might be a good idea to lighten the effect with some late eighteenth-century (or Victorian if you can get them, but they are very difficult to find) glass salt cellars and nice ebony or ivory modern pepper mills. Nevertheless, let us consider silver salts and peppers because there are all sorts of ways of creating a good and happy balance.

If you do decide to have silver salts, now is the time to relate these to that flatware and perhaps the candlesticks that you now have. If you chose the simplicity of fiddle pattern, it might be best to keep most of the other things to relatively simple forms, too.

The chances are quite reasonable that you may have some salts in a velvet-lined, black leather box made at about the turn of the century. If so you are in luck, and you could put these to good use. If, however, these are the salts that you have been used to all your life and feel like going a bit earlier and getting some eighteenth-century salts, the first thing that will strike you is the comparative sizes between salts of this century, notably the early part of this century, compared with earlier examples. The same to a large extent holds true with pepper and sugar castors; not only are they generally much larger than their later counterparts but the holes are comparatively enormous. This was because the pepper and sugar were so much more coarsely ground and the larger holes were needed for the grains to sprinkle out at all, whereas when the same pepper and sugar castors are in use today with the normal fine white pepper, it cascades out! If you use a coarse crystalline rock salt, as I do, it is much easier to see the need for the larger salt cellar employed in the eighteenth century than it is if you use the normal 'table' salt.

One problem with salt is that it corrodes silver and in a few of the damper

A really pretty silver-gilt sugar basin and cream jug made in London in the 1820s. The sugar basin's finial, which is a butterfly sitting on a rose, is such a delightful concept. Worth about £800-1,000.

parts of some country houses I have seen some fairly appalling sights of salt left to sit in a salt cellar for months, maybe years, until as an object, the salt cellar is absolutely beyond redemption. This, of course, is one very good reason for using glass salt cellars but it only needs a modicum of care and commonsense to prevent this happening. It should be stressed that whether your salts are gilded on the inside (salt does not attack gold) or whether they have blue glass liner, the salt should be removed once a week, without fail (and more often in damp and steamy weather) and all given a good wash and thoroughly dried before recharging with salt. Not really a very difficult or arduous operation.

Neither sugar nor pepper attack silver but it is a good idea to do the same with them if only to keep the grains (again, particularly in damp weather) from forming into an immovable block at the bottom of the castor!

Novelty silver objects began to be made during the last half of the nineteenth century and the first quarter of this century, when great strides were made in manufacturing techniques. Mordan & Co made the most astonishing novelties, and particularly notable are the silver and gilt pencils. These can come in every conceivable form including screws, telephone boxes, pillar boxes, and dice. Almost anything could be made into a propelling pencil by this innovative and imaginative firm. Not long ago I saw a collection of over 50 of these pencils and not one was a duplicate! Prices for these pencils can range from £40 to over £200 depending on the ingenuity of the design.

A group of three finely engraved boxes of the 1720s or early 1730s. Wonderful items to collect, and worth about £1,500 each.

Novelty spoon warmers were another craze (a more useless object would be hard to imagine). These were generally made in electro-plate and came in the most enchanting array of disguises, with a frequent use of marine subjects, but many others as well. Another dotty Victorian novelty I came across was a combination cigar lighter, cigar cutter and match box (or, more correctly, vesta box), which I found ingenious and typical of the sense of humour displayed by Victorian artists.

The Victorian Britannia Metal tea or coffee pot comes in a close second after the spoon or fork. These were made in hundreds of thousands to form the large tea and coffee services which were so popular in nineteenth-century England. Although generally now separated from their companion pieces, and despite the poor material from which they are made, many seem to have survived. Most are in a sort of French rococo revival style with baluster body decorated with heavy foliate encrustation. But, however fine they look, the tell-tale mark EPBM (Electro Plate Britannia Metal) on the underneath means they will not be worth very much money. Britannia Metal is an alloy basically similar to pewter which the Victorians found would receive electro-plating just as well as nickel, and at a lower cost. Its disadvantage is its softness and very low melting point, making it prone to damage and difficult to repair with conventional metal solders.

Electro-plate differs considerably from what is generally called Old Sheffield plate and indeed its relative cheapness to manufacture brought about the rapid demise of the earlier, more elaborate, plating system. Old Sheffield plate consisted of fusing a very thin sheet of silver on to a thicker sheet of copper and then working it in the same manner as silver, that is to say raising it with the hammer for hollow-ware or stamping it in a die for candlestick parts and the like. Electro-plate on the other hand was a process of using nickel in any pre-formed shape. The object is then placed in a bath containing a cyanide solution and, with the use of electrodes, a deposit of silver can be laid on to it. That is, of course, vastly over-simplifying the process, but in essence this is how it works.

As it wears, Old Sheffield plate has an increasing amount of copper-coloured metal showing through the silver, whereas with electro-plate one sees only the slightly yellower colour of the nickel showing through. There were many famous makers of very interesting and elaborate objects of electro-plate in the latter part of the last century but perhaps Elkington & Co are the most famous and most innovative. Their work, though generally despised as Victorian electro-plated rubbish only a few years ago, is today much collected and understood for its imagination, vitality and inventiveness, not to mention its fine technical quality.

Elkington's devised a system of date letters and it is thus possible to date their work exactly. On many other pieces the original date of the design can be ascertained by the registration mark, a diamond-shaped mark from which, if you have a de-coder, it is possible to find out not only the year but also the day and the month when the particular design was registered or patented.

There are in this later period many objects of great fun and ingenuity that can readily be found and bought today. There are also, of course, things in quite dreadful bad taste or just simply poor reproductions of another era, but if you have a discerning eye it is possible to find much from the era of our parents and grandparents in which it is worth taking more than a passing interest.

CLEANING SILVER

If you do begin collecting silver, you will also take on the whole business of keeping it clean. Now, I wish to stress the work 'clean' and abjure the word 'polish'. I polish furniture but clean the silver. Indeed, if, whenever you use your silver you follow that by washing it in good hot water then drying it with a tea towel, this will be all it requires for most of the time. However, from time to time a certain amount of tarnish does begin to be noticeable on the surface and

The quintessentially simple English tankard of the seventeenth century. This one was made in Warminster in Wiltshire at about 1685-90, and is worth about £4,000-4,500.

this is when a clean with some proprietary silver cleaner will be necessary. I do not wish to endorse one silver cleaner over another but I would only say that for cleaning rather than polishing silver I find the best, by far and away, to be Goddard's Silver Foam. This wine-coloured sludge comes in a pot with its own sponge and is used in conjunction with water. You also need a soft, preferably badger-hair toothbrush, liquid soap and hot water.

With the sponge and, where necessary, with the toothbrush, clean all over the surface of the object, then remove all the pink paste under running water. Then wash in hot soapy water (with a bit of ammonia if you can stand it), rinse again, and if there is any decoration rinse and scrub with the toothbrush to get every bit of the cleanser out. Finally, dry while the piece is still nice and hot from the water. Simple, yet effective!

In this brief chapter I have really only scratched the surface of the work of silver and plate, but I hope it has inspired you to collect. Who knows, you may soon join the small and exclusive ranks of the permanently poor; poor because you can never afford the necessities of life because you have just spent all remaining money on a frivolity! In short you have become a collector, the bank manager's despair but the romantic's dream.

PAINTINGS

by David Mason

The most important aspect when buying paintings is to buy what you like and what you feel you can live with as opposed to buying 'names'. It is a better investment by far to have the finest example by a minor artist than a minor example by an important name.

The test for any picture that you have bought is of course time, for good pictures grow on you and poor pictures look worse as time goes on, at which point you start to see the faults in the picture and then cannot wait to replace it with something better. Always, therefore, buy the very best that you can afford, and collectors are well advised to have one fine picture rather than ten mediocre pictures. This is, however, more easily said than done. I often come across clients who, when beginning to collect paintings, feel that as they have so many places to fill on their walls and, for example £5,000 to spend, decide to buy ten pictures at £500 each rather than one good picture for £5,000. My advice would be for them to hang nine good prints in the other positions until such time as they can afford another choice example.

The golden rule is always to seek the advice of experts before making a purchase, particularly in auction rooms. It is amazing how many people will go into an auction room and bid for a picture without first having it checked out. This is extremely foolhardy as well as risky. The same people would not dream of buying a house without first having it surveyed. An expert will be able to advise on the authenticity, condition, investment potential and, above all, value of the painting.

VALUING A PAINTING

In many ways pictures can be valued by experts as easily as houses can be valued by estate agents – in each case there are many deciding factors. Let us take the example of a detached house overlooking a railway line, with the rear facing north, which would be valued at, say, £50,000. The same detached house facing south, and overlooking beautiful countryside with a river in the distance, on the other hand, would be worth perhaps as much as 40 per cent more for obvious reasons.

The same criteria apply to pictures. A fine landscape by FW Watts, for instance, with a view of Dedham, showing a beautiful sunny landscape with water, and figures and horses may be worth £100,000, whereas a similar-sized example by the same artist of an enclosed landscape with no water, may be worth only £20,000.

Similarly, if one views the works of the still life and fruit painter, Edward Ladell, the inclusion of a wine glass or silver in a composition would approximately double its value. A Munning's landscape without horses could well be purchased for £10,000, yet a similar-sized landscape with racehorses could well be in the region of £100,000.

These examples are easy to follow and show some of the routes by which paintings are valued: other criteria of course, are condition, quality, period and size of the painting. If the condition is poor, the quality was not the artist's best, the period was towards the end of his life when he may have been a sick man, and the size of the painting is too monstrous for today's houses, the value of the picture will be dramatically affected.

On the following pages I have intentionally avoided being too specific with regard to prices. Although various art indexes are published each year, they only offer an overall guide since they do not mention condition or offer advice on whether the paintings referred to were of a better period or subject.

If a painting is dirty and has a network of crazy paving across the surface, this in itself will not necessarily be detrimental to the value of the painting. These cracks – known as craquelure – are caused over a long period by the medium beneath the oil painting drying out. By a process of relining, the canvas can be fused to the original which will close these cracks so that they become almost imperceptible. To the lay person considering the purchase of an obviously old painting, the advice must be to refer to an expert who will be able to tell you whether the painting can be satisfactorily restored.

It is worth remembering that the restorer will charge you the same for working on an indifferent painting purchased for a couple of hundred pounds, as for a fine work that may be worth £80,000. Hence it is only worth buying a painting seemingly in a bad state if you can justify the cost of restoration, which may run into many hundreds of pounds. It might be that only a minimum of restoration is required and only an expert will be able to recognise this beneath perhaps a hundred years' accumulated dirt and old varnish.

Filippo Baratti,
Whitehall, (*signed and dated 1884*).

FREDERICK WATERS WATTS 1800-1862
'A Country Lane Near Dedham'
Oil on canvas 100cm (40in) x 150cm (54¾in)

We all have personal preferences and it is with this in mind that my selection of paintings should present a group of contrasting subjects, offering differing styles of painting.

Whilst some buyers look for a great degree of detail in the drawing of figures, buildings or ships, others will be attracted to a broader style, offering more suggestions of form. Frederick Waters Watts' painting of the River Stour, known to us all as Constable country, falls very much into the latter category. Born in 1800, just 24 years after John Constable, there is no record of the two artists ever meeting, yet the influence of Constable on the younger Watts is unmistakable.

Artists of the nineteenth century tended to seek a greater degree of naturalism in their work than their somewhat more formal predecessors of the eighteenth century, and Watts expresses this tendency very well.

Painters of the English landscape, if confined to the nineteenth century, were almost legion and, whilst you might pay £100,000 for the best example by Watts, by scouring the market you will be able to find a very wide range of artists whose work can still be bought for comparatively modest prices.

EUGENE DE BLAAS 1843-1931
'The New Suitor'
Signed
Oil on canvas 98cm (35in) x 116cm (42½in)

Eugene de Blaas was one of the most well-known Italian painters of the nineteenth century and is a particular favourite of mine. This painting embodies all that is good in figure painting – vitality, freshness, spontaneity and colour. I chose this painting for inclusion in one of the *Heirloom* programmes because it offers a lesson in what to look for. The condition of a painting is never more important than when looking at figure paintings. Even from this small illustration you can see the detail in the drawing of the hands, the lovely flesh tints, the clever contrasts in the skirts and the rougher texture of the man's trousers, and again the textures of the old bricks and the copper milk buckets. Be it a single portrait or a painting of many figures like this one, if it is cleaned badly it will lose some of its glazes. Once they have gone they cannot be replaced by the restorer.

With regard to pricing a painting such as this, I think the best advice I can give is to visit as many galleries as possible so that, in comparing prices, you will very soon be able to make your own comparisons and the right judgment. (This is also relevant when looking at lesser-priced work.) Generally, though, the work of Eugene de Blaas may range in value from £10,000 to over £100,000.

FREDERIK MARIANUS KRUSEMAN 1816-1882
'Skaters on a Frozen Canal'
Signed and dated 1857
Oil on canvas 80cm (29in) x 115cm (41in)

The flat landscape and low horizon of Holland made necessary a certain approach to the composition of a painting. I think this is particularly well illustrated by FM Kruseman who is a great favourite among collectors of the Dutch nineteenth-century painters of landscapes. Kruseman was particularly good at painting winter scenes, a difficult and challenging subject. Two-thirds of the canvas is sky and Kruseman's unique ability was to use the sky and wonderful clouds to great effect. Unlike many of his contemporaries he also painted figures extremely well.

The average size painting by this artist may today command a figure in excess of £70,000. If you purchase a painting of a similar view, but by a minor artist, you will find that the snow does not have the same conviction nor does the sky radiate the same light.

A well-balanced painting gives years of pleasure whilst a crudely painted or imbalanced composition is a reminder of a less successful purchase, hence my advice is to view as many paintings as possible before committing yourself.

HARRY HALL 1838-1886
'Underhand' Winner of the Northumberland Plate with Aldcroft Up,
Mr A Biggs, Mr J Fobart (Trainer) and Mr G Foster (Owner)
Signed and dated 1860
Oil on canvas 98cm (35in) x 196cm (50in)

Though racing may still be the sport of kings, I am sure there cannot be many families in the country that do not have a member interested in the sport. It goes back to Saxon times and by the reign of Charles I races were being held in Hyde Park and Newmarket. The Jockey Club was established by 1752 at Newmarket and soon to follow were a lot of the races known today: Goodwood was established by the Duke of Richmond, and the most famous flat race, the Derby, by the 12th Earl.

I have selected a painting not by the eighteenth-century painter George Stubbs, whose name we would all be familiar with, nor the nineteenth-century John Frederick Herring Senior, but a similar work by Harry Hall. It is typical of its period when the owners loved to show their favourite horses painted with the jockey, trainer and portraits of themselves.

You can spend hundreds of thousands of pounds on important paintings of racing but it is still possible to buy views of the single racehorse in its loosebox or racing scenes for a few thousand pounds. This illustrates, as do so many subjects, the dilemma of the buyer as to whether to go for a number of lesser-priced paintings or one by a better artist and better quality. Whether you are looking at horses or landscapes, try to view as many paintings as possible and your eye will soon become tuned to quality. If you are going to commit some of your capital for a period of ten years, the best painting invariably gives the best return. This sort of painting would sell for £40-60,000.

FRANCIS HOLMAN ?-1790
'British Men o'War off the Coast'
Oil on canvas 100cm (36in) x 148cm (54in)

As an island nation dependent upon trade, our history has linked us inextricably with the sea. It was from the sixteenth and seventeenth centuries that the real foundations of our marine school were laid, but for collecting I think the majority of us tend to buy eighteenth- or nineteenth-century work. Francis Holman, the English artist whose painting I have chosen, recorded naval actions and the Thames dockyards besides more general scenes. This particular painting to me illustrates the lovely drawing that the artists of the time achieved.

Of paramount importance to the buyer of paintings of this age is, of course, condition, for it is the fine detail around the hulls and rigging where the paintings would have suffered in 200 years if they had been badly cleaned.

I cannot over-emphasise this point because even small examples of either eighteenth-century or nineteenth-century marine paintings will sell for £5-10,000, whilst the larger, more important works command sums of between £30-80,000. Often the artists showed different elevations of the same vessel or, as Holman has done with this painting, various sail rigs, furled, then on the left the ship approaching you with shortened sails, whilst on the right you see the stern view with all sails set.

There are many artists of marine painting from the last 200 years to choose from and this type of painting has always been and will surely remain a most popular subject.

HENRY ALKEN SENIOR 1785-1851
'The Meet'
Oil on canvas 33cm (12in) x 40cm (16in)

As with racing, the roots of hunting date back to Saxon times. One interesting aspect of the sport is that in the eighteenth century, the time of John Wootton and John Nost Sartorious, the scenes they painted were often set in wooded summer landscapes. Today hunting is a winter pastime and it was not until the reign of George II that hunting was forbidden until after the harvest.

As a general guide, the 'rocking horse' painting – showing the horse at a gallop with all four legs fully extended – survived until the turn of the nineteenth century. I have selected a painting by Henry Alken because he introduced humour into his paintings. His well-known engravings of the 'Miseries of Shooting' and 'The Right Sort' showed that disasters can befall both horse and rider.

We are all familiar with the engravings that adorn the walls of the English pub or country hotel and if you are buying these, be sure to go to a well-known gallery that will advise you on the different engravings and whether they are original or modern hand-coloured prints; for one may be worth just a few pounds and the original coloured engravings a few thousand. To the untrained eye it is difficult to differentiate between one and the other. If you are a prospective buyer of the oil paintings, some of the contemporary English artists are worth considering, both artistically and financially. This sort of painting would be worth around £30-50,000, depending on size and quality.

EDWARD LADELL 1821-1886
'A Still Life of Fruit, A Basket and A Wine Glass'
Signed with monogram
Oil on canvas 37cm (14in) x 33cm (12in)

Holland of the seventeenth century is generally regarded as the home of the great painters of flower and still life paintings, but in the main my group of paintings are nineteenth century and to illustrate this subject I have therefore selected a painting by an English artist of the nineteenth century named Edward Ladell. I have sold many paintings by this artist and I believe the great attraction to collectors is the inimitable way he managed to paint the bloom on the grapes, and the clever composition he achieved on comparatively small canvases that captured the light as it fell across different textures and surfaces. If you look closely at the illustration you can see the reflections in the glass; the outline is clear and defined and you feel you can almost touch the fruit.

A painting such as the one illustrated may be worth between £25-30,000 in good condition, but this could be reduced to less than half if in poor condition.

MONTAGUE DAWSON 1895-1973
'The Night Watch'
Oil on canvas 54cm (20in) x 85cm (30in)

I have chosen the above painting by Montague Dawson because it illustrates the fundamental change in the approach to the sea between that painted by artists of the eighteenth century and the work of an artist in the mid-twentieth century. (The former was rather regulated, whereas the latter is more natural.)

Depicting the great tea clippers were subjects that made Dawson's name famous. Where a large painting of his could have been purchased in the early 1960s for a few thousand pounds, that same painting may today be worth between £50-70,000. I think the artist's great talent was that you can imagine yourself on board the deck of the clipper and appreciate the condition of the seas shown in his paintings. Dawson did not date his paintings but, as a guide, the seas in his earlier work were less free in style.

Dawson painted in watercolour but these do not generally compare with the price structure of his oil paintings of the clipper, battle scenes or the best of his yachting, which have greatly increased in popularity in recent years.

Many will remember the painting he did of Sir Francis Chichester rounding the Horn in 'Gipsy Moth' in the 1960s; this and a number of his other paintings have been published as signed limited editions. At auctions devoted entirely to reproductions these prints sell for many hundreds of pounds. If you are buying these, make sure they bear the stamp of the Fine Art Guild.

FEDERICO DEL CAMPO
'A View of the Grand Canal, Venice'
Signed
Oil on canvas 48cm (18in) x 72cm (27in)

There could hardly be a city in the world more painted than Venice, and this picture I find especially appealing. Improbable as it may seem, Federico del Campo, who painted the picture illustrated, was born in Lima in Peru, and yet his name was to become synonymous with Venice.

Whilst the painters of the eighteenth century were essentially draughtsmen, by the 1880s the very approach of the artists had changed. The result was one of vibrance through the use of colour and, above all, the understanding and command of light. This picture is a good example of this new approach of painting. It must have been the abundance of scenes that caught the artists' imaginations: the combination of canals, churches and palaces. This sort of painting would be worth around £60-80,000.

FURNITURE

by John Bly

Old furniture, by its very nature, is probably more prone to alteration and 'improvement' than any other type of antique. Its history is full of revivals in style and reconstructions in body, of later decorative enrichment, enthusiastic restoration and even, dare we say it, faking! But it is these very characteristics, coupled with the possible discovery of some rare and wonderful authentic piece, that make antique furniture such a fascinating subject.

A mid-eighteenth-century oak dressing table or 'lowboy', just early enough in design to be later decorated with walnut veneers and pass as authentic. This type of oak furniture was poorly regarded until recent years, and so in the early 1900s such improvement was not considered too dreadful. So beware: the price difference between the original plain oak, the later veneered and the authentic walnut piece is many thousands of pounds.

Most of us own furniture from the late Victorian or Edwardian periods, *circa* 1875-1910. During this time the styles of all previous periods were popular, and mechanical mass-production made it possible to supply the tremendous demand. The designs of Chippendale, Hepplewhite and Sheraton were adapted and modified to create new furniture with the 'antique' look – although it was not called that at the time. Unfortunately, perhaps when some new furniture was more than a family could afford, original old heirlooms were brought up to date by the addition of carving and inlay. This old furniture was of the plain run-of-the-mill sort. It was plentiful and cheap, and its improvement, after 80 or 90 years' wear and tear, has created quite a hazard for the collector today. So it is not surprising that most of the furniture selected for the *Heirloom* programme will have a story to tell. One example is the walnut bureau cabinet that appeared to be a genuine Queen Anne piece until close scrutiny revealed that it was basically an authentic but plain oak example, later decorated with fine walnut veneers. Naturally the owner was disappointed at the news, but he brightened up when told that the value would still be in the region of £20,000! (An original would be over three times that amount!)

It takes quite a bit of practice to give a positive diagnosis like that, but it sounds more complicated than it really is. There are some basic ground rules to be followed, rather like a checklist, in order to establish authenticity or reasons for doubt and it can be the greatest possible fun to play detective and piece together the whys and wherefores of the alteration or 'improvement'. First we have to establish that the form, use, material and construction are all compatible with the age the item purports to be. There could not be, for example, a genuine 1630s' full-length dressing mirror in a satinwood swing frame, glued and screwed together and decorated with woven cane panels, because none of those things had been invented, used, made or discovered by that date. It helps if we bear in mind the evolution of shapes and timbers used.

DIFFERENT STYLES OF FURNITURE

Good furniture from the second half of the seventeenth century was flamboyant, sometimes to the point of being fussy, and was made of oak or walnut in the solid. The same quality Queen Anne furniture at the beginning of the eighteenth century was softer, rounder, generally curvilinear and often decorated with walnut veneers. The early Georgian era, up to the 1760s, saw a return to great flamboyance in the French rococo style with mahogany as the primary timber. The late Georgian period, from the last quarter of the eighteenth century, through the Regency period and up to 1830 began with a strong influence from ancient classical architecture, creating the great age of elegance, and ended with a revival of the 'Old French' of the seventeenth and eighteenth centuries. Gothic and Chinese were two other styles which remained popular, and the import of exotic timbers such as satinwood, rosewood, amboyna and coromandel, used mainly as veneers, added variety to the surface treatment. After the 1830s styles ceased to go completely 'out of fashion'; they just ran on to be joined by revivals or innovations, like the taste for the mock Tudor and Elizabethan styles so popularised by the writings of Sir Walter Scott.

Thus the Victorian period saw an invasion of styles and materials, with oak and walnut returning to favour, one piling on top of another until the 1890s when the revivals of Chippendale, Hepplewhite and Sheraton led the way into the twentieth century.

The Arts and Crafts Movement, founded in the early 1860s, was an important alternative new style, born out by its later and more familiar name 'Art Nouveau'. It was sometimes sombre, sometimes sinuous, often controversial and always eye-catching. It was intended to be pure, craftsman-made and unsullied by mechanisation but handmade production costs were prohibitively high and, to meet the demand, machine manufacture eventually defeated the Movement's primary objectives with cheap imitations.

It seems hard to believe that until the 1890s genuine antique furniture was by no means as popular as it is today. There were few true collectors and connoisseurship was in its infancy. In fact, as late as the 1870s there were still shops in London's Soho where Elizabethan and earlier furniture could be bought for breaking up to be rebuilt into pieces more suitable for the modern home. It is from this category that so many disappointments occur today, for in the construction of such treasured pieces a predominance of old timber and a hundred years or so of daily use can be very convincing on grandfather's oak sideboard, court-cupboard or monk's bench. The creation of such pastiches added considerably to the already enormous machine-assisted production of monstrously carved oak Renaissance-style cupboards, dressers, benches and so on, throughout England, the Continent of Europe, and America, which is why we see so much furniture in this style today.

A mahogany side chair *circa* 1880 in the Queen Anne/George I style. Although deceptively faithful to the original design at first glance, the seat frame is too shallow to date from the early eighteenth century. Even if all the proportions were correct for that period, the use of mahogany would not be compatible. Nevertheless, the chair is of fine quality and just old enough to be an antique in its own right. As a guide to price, this chair would be valued in the low hundreds of pounds, whereas the eighteenth-century walnut version would be in the thousands.

A late nineteenth-century mahogany display cabinet in the 'Chinese Chippendale' style. Fine quality furniture like this was made well into the twentieth century and, although not yet strictly antique, has enjoyed a justifiable increase in appreciation and price during recent years, now heading well into four figures. (The original eighteenth-century version would be well into five figures.) The primary element that indicates nineteenth rather than eighteenth-century date is the over-slender proportion of the legs.

ESTABLISHING AUTHENTICITY

Obviously the Victorian period is a complicated one for the antique collector, but we do have the advantage of the large number of contemporary trade and showroom catalogues, published by leading manufacturers and suppliers to illustrate the latest 'lines' and models. More specifically they show us how the nineteenth-century criteria for proportion and design differ from the preceding periods. Also important are the catalogues of the fabulous international exhibitions which were staged in most major cities worldwide following the first and most influential of all, the Great Exhibition of 1851. Housed in a huge structure of glass designed by Robert Paxton and justly named the Crystal Palace, it was without doubt responsible for the awakening of interest in the decorative arts among the public in general throughout the land. The illustrated catalogue to the Great Exhibition shows furniture and works of art from all over the world, which gave new ideas to manufacturers and consumers at every level. Among the new and revitalised materials for the furniture industry was papier mâché.

Papier mâché was originally made popular in England during the latter half of the eighteenth century by Henry Clay, and later by the firm of Jennens and Bettridge. It was first used to make small and decorative objects like trays and wine coasters. By the 1840s, however, the imaginative Victorians had adopted the material to make chairs, tables and even beds, as well as every conceivable box, casket, inkstand or novelty piece you could ever need or wish to collect. It was even reported that an entire village was made of papier mâché, but that was in Australia where presumably the climate was kinder to the material than our English rain might have been.

One of a set of three magazine and paper racks, made of mass-produced papier mâché. The simulated tortoiseshell background and the eighteenth-century-style costumes are typical of the last quarter of the nineteenth century. By the time these racks were made the papier mâché industry was on the decline. Examples from this period must be in good condition to be of any commercial value today. This set is worth about £400-600.

Early papier mâché, that is dating from the 1780s through to the 1830s, is very collectable and can be worth a great deal of money, particularly if it is signed by the maker. But such pieces are scarce and most examples will date from after the 1850s when production was at its height and the merchandise was cheap enough to be within the reach of most people.

Quality and condition vary considerably and will govern today's market price. As the supply was so huge it is possible to be selective and an idea for a collection is to pick the work of one particular decorator, like William Jackson, best known for his wonderful paintings of lilies-of-the-valley, or choose a specific type of article such as the wine coaster, pen-tray or tea caddy. Deep black is the normal background but primary colours were used, and examples of these are at a premium.

To help approximate dating of papier mâché we use some of the well-chronicled developments in the history of the industry. For example, in 1825 George Souter, who worked for Jennens and Bettridge, introduced the application of thin slips of mother-of-pearl on to a papier mâché surface, so such decoration will be after that date. Some years later the same firm introduced the use of aluminium powder, and after 1860 surfaces made to look like tortoise-shell and malachite became particularly popular. The paper rack shown opposite is an example of this type.

Tunbridgeware is another type of decoration which became very much a vogue by the 1830s. As the name suggests, the centre for its production was Tunbridge, where the local water stained certain timbers green and novelty souvenirs had been produced as a result for many years. The effect of Tunbridge decoration is similar in appearance to that of mosaic work, using tiny sections of contrasting coloured woods. This is achieved by creating the desired picture with strips of timber, rather like long matchsticks, gluing them together to form a block and finally cutting slices off the end to create pieces of veneer.

A panel of Tunbridgeware decoration. The appearance is similar to mosaic work, but the construction is very different. What you see are the ends of strips of wood, like long matchsticks, glued together in picture formation to make a block. Thin slices are cut vertically from this block to create the veneer panels and borders.

Among the most common objects to be decorated in this way were boxes to contain gloves, tea, stamps or needlework, or the larger ones made to fold as portable writing or 'lap' desks. Many of these have a small brass plaque set into the lid, sometimes bearing engraved initials or, even better, a presentation inscription giving us an accurate date and a fascinating insight into its family heirloom history. At least one tea caddy or lap desk is included in every *Heirloom* series for just that reason – the box may be quite ordinary, but its documented story makes it unique. The most common type of decorative pattern is the geometric ribbon border, while sprays of flowers and scenes of stately homes, both real and imaginary, are among the most desirable.

Berlin needlework is a third decorative art form which affected the furniture industry during the nineteenth century. Basically comprising a DIY package of picture printed with colour guide and all the requisite wools, Berlin needlework became the hobby for every young girl in the country, if the amount extant today is anything to go by! The package was first imported from Berlin in the early 1800s, and by 1840 it was possible to choose from some 14,000 different patterns. Everything from wall hangings to slippers were subject to the medium, but it is the panels for fire screens, trays and tabletops which are of interest to the furniture collector. A fine example of such a piece is shown below, and illustrates the most superb quality stand in solid rosewood.

We always have a large selection of Berlin work to choose from when preparing the *Heirloom* programme and once again it is the story behind the piece which will make our decision. The value is determined by quality, preservation of colour, general condition and subject matter – religious scenes are not the best of sellers. As a rough guide to dating Berlin work, remember that the earliest examples were fairly simple in design and material content, whereas the later, post-1840 packages incorporated a variety of stitches, primary colours and additional materials, like glass beads.

Decorative carving or inlaying authentic but originally plain furniture of the Chippendale and Sheraton periods was a common practice in Victorian times. Whether done for innocent or fraudulent reasons the result is the same: an item less than totally genuine but interesting and now even collectable in its own right. Of course, the difference in price between the original and the altered piece can run into thousands of pounds and so for this reason alone it is essential to be able to recognise one from the other. A good guide to later carving is whether or not the decoration stands proud of the outline. Remember that most furniture from the eighteenth century was made plain. When an article was intended to be carved the maker allowed sufficient timber for the carver to execute his designs in such a way that

An early Victorian pole-screen, the tripod stand of solid rosewood supporting a banner of Berlin needlework. Both are of fine quality and well preserved. This is particularly important where Berlin work is concerned, for the coloured wools have often faded badly, drastically reducing the value today. Subject matter is also important; religious scenes are more difficult to sell than secular ones at the moment. Worth about £1,800-2,200.

they appeared as additional to the form or shape of the piece. When an article was intended to be plain, no such allowance of extra timber was made and any subsequent carving had to be within the existing outline.

The same principles can be applied to furniture of the Sheraton period; most of it was originally plain. Only the finest was decorated with inlay of marquetry panels depicting fans, seashells, scrolls, musical instruments and classical motifs. But by 1900 such panels were being mass-produced and sold to furniture restorers and cabinet-makers all over the country, to be 'let in' to the surfaces or erstwhile plain tables, sideboards, cabinets, bureaux and chairs. Where this has happened, however, the surface will usually show some indentation in the newly worked area when viewed obliquely against the light. It is also important to bear in mind the question of whether the piece would have been sufficiently important to have warranted expensive decoration in the first place.

A fine mid-eighteenth-century mahogany tea or 'silver' table, so named because it often held the silver tea service. Today this is a valuable collectors' item, its value in the high thousands, and to alter it in any way would be sacrilege; but 90 years or so ago it was just the sort of plain piece that a carver might have 'improved' with scrolls to the knees and leaf capping to each foot. However, all such later decoration will appear within the outline of the curves, while original carving will stand proud of the surface.

The shape or form of a piece can sometimes make it possible for you to identify it as being Victorian or Edwardian, a fine example being the illustration overleaf. It is a type of writing desk, actually combining the main elements of three established pieces of furniture: the upper part from a Bonheur du jour (a lady's writing table), the middle from a cylinder-fall writing desk, and the base from a davenport. Both the Bonheur du jour and the small cylinder-fall desk were popular in England after the 1780s and are usually attributed to designs by Thomas Sheraton. The davenport is said to have got its name from a Captain Davenport who first commissioned such a piece from Gillows of Lancaster (later Waring and Gillow). While the use of rosewood veneer and inlay of marquetry would have been compatible with the late eighteenth century, the combination of those three different pieces of furniture certainly would not. Closer inspection of the marquetry confirms a late date, for the quality of design and execution are well below that of the original.

Given various changes in style and decoration the Bonheur du jour and the davenport remained popular throughout the nineteenth century, with the davenport showing the greatest increase in value, particularly in recent years. A fine 'piano' top model, that is one with a curving rather than flat schooldesk-type lid, in good condition and with fine colour walnut veneers, can fetch in excess of £2,000.

It is curious how one may see something for the first time and then encounter another soon after. This happened to me in the last *Heirloom* series with an Irish davenport, the like of which I had never seen before. It was bigger in every

Left This fine quality, late nineteenth-century writing desk actually combines major elements from three popular late eighteenth-century pieces of furniture. Worth about £3,500-4,500.

Right A close-up of the marquetry panel inlaid on the front of the desk. Even if the desk was earlier than the late nineteenth century the marquetry certainly was not! The Roman vase motif flanked by Greek key pattern handles was not a popular combination in the eighteenth century.

dimension than the standard size and smothered with wonderful marquetry depicting flowers, scrolls, cottages and rural scenes and, naturally, a harp. It had secret drawers and compartments and the owners told of its interesting history. They, too, had never seen one like it. During the next week I was called out to see some furniture in my home town and there was the twin davenport! Stranger still, the following week a third turned up in a London saleroom. Likewise, the auctioneer had never seen one; so I wonder how many were made, where they are, and if I shall find one for another programme!

Of course, not all revival styles should be thought of as causing problems for today's enthusiast. Far from it. Many can be seen as a welcome expansion on established patterns. The international exhibitions had created a certain demand for French, Italian, Spanish and Moorish styles in modern as well as traditional interpretation.

Black and gold decoration – among the most popular Continental influences of the nineteenth century – found favour on a wide range of furniture. An ingenious example of this type was shown in an *Heirloom* programme last year. It was a rectangular table on four turned and tapering legs. The whole surface was ebonised and lightened with gouged, gilded lines and some fine quality gilt metal mounts. The double top lifted and swivelled round in the nineteenth-century manner to form a baize-covered card table. But underneath the lower leaf there was a complete fitted dressing table with adjustable mirror. Although this was no surprise to the owner, it was to me – and to the audience! So, too, would be today's valuation of well over £3,000!

Metal mounts on furniture can reveal a great deal. Take castors for example. These little wheels came into common use during the mid-eighteenth century, although they were a much earlier invention. To facilitate moving the furniture without cutting the carpet, castors of the 1750s are usually smaller in diameter than in width, and made up of several leather washers fixed together. The wheels of brass castors – which gradually replaced the leather ones – were at first of the same wide, squat proportion, but by the 1790s they had become thinner and larger in diameter. Like the furniture, they became more elegant. During the Victorian period porcelain and stoneware castor wheels were introduced, so if you see those on a piece of eighteenth-century furniture, they must be replacements.

Locks, hinges and handles were also very much part of the furniture industry by the early part of the eighteenth century, and fixing screws too can provide a useful guide to authenticity. Until the early nineteenth century steel screws (which had been in use for about 100 years by then) were cut by hand, and the tops finished with a file. When they were machine-made the finishing was done on a mill and the tops look like a miniature gramophone record. If you see this spun effect on the head of a screw it is unlikely to be eighteenth century.

A type of filigree veneer, an ancient decorative technique which first found favour in England in the early 1700s, was revived in the nineteenth century using brass and tortoiseshell. It was introduced and developed by André

Left A mid-Victorian walnut-veneered combined Canterbury and whatnot. The exuberance of the decoration is typical of the 1860s and shows the high quality attainable by skilled machine-carvers. Accurate dating is possible by reference to contemporary catalogues (*above*). Finding an example which compares so closely is always exciting. Worth about £2,000-2,500.

Charles Boulle and has ever since carried his name. (An alternative spelling is Buhl.) The method of manufacture is similar to that of marquetry wherein a sheet of each material is glued one to the other and a design cut through with a fine saw. When the sheets are separated, one panel will drop into the other to create two decorative panels: one with a tortoiseshell design in a brass background, the other vice versa. Thus most boulle-decorated pieces were made in pairs and their decoration known as boulle and contre-boulle. Eighteenth-century examples are rare and terribly expensive, whereas the nineteenth-century pieces were made on a large scale and, while still costly, are certainly available. One guide to the difference is the thickness of the veneer. Until the nineteenth century all veneers – wood, metal, ivory, tortoiseshell or whatever – had to be cut by hand-saw. This meant a minimum thickness of approximately 10mm (1/6in) could be achieved. After the development of mechanisation the same veneers could be produced to a paper-thin gauge. This is not quite so easy to assess on wood veneers but boulle is highly prone to movement and damage, and so where some brass or tortoiseshell has blistered or popped up, that is the place to look. If it is very thin it is most likely to be of nineteenth-century origin rather than earlier.

Quality is one of the most important aspects to consider when evaluating the worth of an item. But degrees of quality are difficult to establish without the opportunity for comparison, and this is one area where the *Heirloom* programme has an advantage. Because of the way the programme is structured it is

Part of the back rail from a Victorian balloon-back chair, showing quite a high standard of machine carving, certainly compared to that opposite. The wood has a good colour that has not been tampered with, the design is well drawn and the scrolls and leaves have some life. The quality of the carving you can see, particularly on upholstered furniture, is often a good guide to the quality of the timber and workmanship that you can't see!

possible to show, hopefully without offending anyone, bad as well as good examples. Look, for instance, at the two chair backs illustrated at the base of this page. Both are machine-carved and date from the 1870s, but the one on the left is clearly superior in quality to the other. It is well drawn, deeply cut to give a good three-dimensional effect, the edges to the scrolls are rounded and fluid, and the background is nicely chased. The other chair back by comparison is an uninspired pattern, the carving is flat and lifeless, and the background is poorly done.

Fine upholstered furniture of the eighteenth century was of somewhat limited supply and is therefore rare today, but the Victorian workshops spawned absolutely masses of chairs, settees, chaises, love seats, stools and all manner of upholstered items. On such furniture the quality of the carving on the parts of the frame you can see will often be a guide to the quality of the parts you cannot see under the upholstery. Remember that cheap furniture made for the mass market relied on cheap materials as well as cheap labour, and much of the wood was already infected with worm or disease when it was used. When buying, selling or restoring this sort of heirloom, do seek some expert advice, for a good button-back parlour chair can be worth the best part of £2,000, while a poor one is less than £200!

Dealing with furniture certainly has its pitfalls, but a little basic knowledge and plenty of enthusiasm will allow anyone to have hours of pleasure just looking at furniture heirlooms.

Part of the back rail from a Victorian balloon-back chair. The frame has been stripped and varnished at some time but even that cannot conceal the poor standard of machine carving. Furniture of this quality filled a gap in the market then, just as it does now, but it should not be mistaken for its better contemporaries, nor considered over-worthy just because it is old, and it certainly should not be over-priced.

TOYS

by Hilary Kay

Children today have their choice of commercially produced toys imported from countries the world over and designed to appeal from the moment their eyes and hands can coordinate. It was not always so, however; the enlightened attitude that children develop skills of coordination and learning through toys and play was not widely accepted until this century.

WOOD AND PAPER TOYS

Some of the earliest and most attractive toys which appear at auction are those made from carved and painted wood. These originated generally in southern Germany and take the form of soldiers and forts, farmyards, market scenes and Noah's arks. These toys would perhaps have been made originally by a father or grandfather for their own children but from the 1850s onwards advances were made in mass-production techniques and the wooden toys began to be made in sufficient numbers to allow export to other European countries. Noah's arks proved to be particularly popular, partly attributable to their more general design, and having fewer direct links through regional costume or style of architecture with the region of south Germany from where they originated.

Noah's arks usually have brightly painted architectural detail and decoration on the hull and superstructure, the roof of the cabin is normally hinged and lifts to reveal the contents of paired birds and beasts ranging from elephants to spiders. Some of the more comprehensive sets of animals found in the larger arks would include such exotic birds and beasts as flamingos and ring-tailed lemurs alongside the more familiar species from the countryside and farmyard. Strict adherence to scale proved to be something of a problem to the carvers – Noah and his family tend to look on amazed as grasshoppers the size of dogs board the craft two by two. The lasting popularity of arks was assured since they were one of the few amusements which, in strictly religious households, children were permitted to play with on the Sabbath. These particular wooden toys appear to have survived in reasonable quantities although they seldom escape without damage to the paint and the delicate legs of the birds and beasts within.

Other amusements which were permitted to be used on a Sunday would have included paper or cardboard games which had particular emphasis on the Christian message. These may have included alphabet or picture blocks printed with recognisable biblical characters or scenes. On a day-to-day basis children would have had a number of educational games to choose from, whether to encourage them to read, spell, add or subtract, or learn about history and geography.

Opposite A large Noah's ark and animals, 59cm (23in) long, made in Germany in the mid-nineteenth century. Worth £400-600.

100

Ivory spelling sets were popular, with the alphabet letters intricately cut and shaped and stored in mahogany boxes, as were 'dissected maps' of the United Kingdom with each county forming a piece from a jig-saw to be slotted into its correct geographical position within the country boundaries. Genealogical games were produced to teach the young scholar about past kings and queens as were amusements designed to show the virtues of leading a good life and the hazards of evil living.

But it was from the last part of the nineteenth century onwards that board games were produced solely for amusement rather than education. From that time until the present day games have been manufactured to reflect the interests of the day and have mirrored contemporary advances in technology and design. Games such as 'The Great Yacht Race' and the 'Motor Race' tell today's collector a great deal about the period in which they were played, just as observers in the future may look at games popular today, such as 'Risk' and 'Wall Street', and wonder at the values and concerns of our post-war society.

Board and table games are still relatively easy to find in salerooms and antique shops and, compared with the increasing popularity of board game collecting in America, in England collectors are few and far between.

A selection of hollow-cast lead soldiers, made by William Britain.

METAL TOYS

With the growth of the industrial revolution during the nineteenth century, the use of machines and machined metal in the production of playthings became increasingly prolific as machined toys could be turned out at prices which would undercut toys of wood and paper which were produced painstakingly by hand.

Some of the earliest manufactured metal toys were flat tin figures produced in a mould. Molton tin was poured into a well-detailed metal template, allowed to cool, and then removed and painted. One company particularly associated with these types of flat tin figures or scenes is that of Ernst Heinrichsen, founded in Nuremberg in 1842. The popularity of the figures produced by Heinrichsen were such that the company continued in business until after the First World War.

Solid figures, also produced from a mould into which the molten alloy was poured, appeared more lifelike and grew in popularity during the latter part of the nineteenth century. Companies such as Heyde, Mignot and Lucotte are particularly associated with the production of these solid figures and soldiers produced in the last century. Figures are still being produced by the Mignot factory today.

But it was the English manufacturer, William Britain, who is best known for his production of lead soldiers. The Britain factory had produced rather interesting lead alloy clockwork toys in the 1880s but it was only when the company used their skills in moulding lead in the 1890s and applied it to producing hollow moulded soldiers that the company achieved popularity. Its wares were of consistently high quality and to a scale large enough for the detailed uniforms of the various regiments of Britain, her Empire and the rest of the world to be easily recognisable, and they were widely collected.

They were retailed in distinctive maroon boxes stating the name of the regiment and, in the case of the early boxes, details of the regiment's outstanding battle achievements in the past. Britain's range of products reflected the advances in warfare technology over the decades, with the evolution from the horse to motorised tanks, personnel carriers and assault vehicles.

After the First World War, perhaps in an attempt to attract girls as well as boys to their products, Britain's began to produce lead garden sets and farmyard accessories which enjoyed a period of great favour between the wars. Britain's farmyards were particularly collected in the 1930s and this has ensured that these toys are possible to find either singly or as larger collections.

The evolution of injection-moulded plastics after the Second World War very largely put an end to the manufacture of moulded lead soldiers and civilian figures, although their popularity in the new material was as strong as ever.

Mechanical metal toys are some of the most desirable and highly prized toys today. They were made in Europe, principally in Germany, and in America from the last quarter of the nineteenth century through until the start of the Second World War.

The earliest mechanical metal toys were brass locomotives powered by steam which was produced by a spirit burner beneath the water reservoir. These early steam engines were often made by manufacturers better known for their production of scientific instruments, such as Newton, and were perhaps created as educational demonstration models rather than designed for the amusement of a child. Movements from clocks were adapted and used in the locomotion of

A 3½-inch gauge brass 2-2-2 locomotive, made in England in the late nineteenth century. Worth £300-500.

toys from the late nineteenth century and by 1900 clockwork toys were being produced in large numbers of factories, principally in Germany.

TINPLATE TOYS

The German companies of Märklin, Bing, Carette, Gunthermann, Plank and Schoenner produced some of the more exciting tinplate toys during the few years just before 1900 up until the First World War. Thin sheets of steel were coated with an even thinner layer of tin to create tinplate; this medium became widely used as the raw material for making toys. Easy to cut and bend into the required shape, simple to solder and with fair resistance to rust, tinplate toys could be shaped initially by machine presses, and then details completed by hand. They were painted in bright colours, which were enamelled on to the tinplate in ovens, and then finished with a thick layer of varnish.

The German manufacturers were particularly adroit at appealing to foreign markets by adapting their products. Very similar battleship designs, for example, were produced by the Märklin company but they would be named to suit their markets – 'Maine' for America, 'Kaiser Willhelm II' for Germany and so on. This targeting for markets can be noticed particularly in the manufacture of toy trains where cow catchers were added for the American market and the actual pressings and livery of the train would change from the Continental style to that of the British railway network with accessories in the style of the country to match: stations, rolling stock, coaches, lamps and bridges all subtly altered to suit.

A Gauge 0 tinplate trainset in original cardboard box, made by Gebrüder Bing in Germany, *circa* 1915. Worth £400-600.

Tinplate toys were expensive even at the time of purchase, with a large tin battleship costing a similar sum to the weekly wage of a doctor at the time. Little wonder that these toys were cherished and children may not have been allowed to play with them without supervision. Despite this, toys were damaged, some through excessive heat if steam-powered; others, by mishap or neglect, became rusty or tatty and many were discarded. This has meant today that toys which were originally scarce through price are now almost impossible to find in good, unrestored condition leading to extremely high prices being attained by out-standing examples.

After the First World War it may have been lack of skilled manpower due to the excessive losses in battle that encouraged the large toy manufacturers to concentrate on further advances in mechanised production techniques. Lithographic printing on to tin had been known for many years but its application in the manufacture of larger tin toys became much more widespread in the period just after the First World War. Sheets of tin were printed with the toy's decorative and structural details, then cut and pressed to shape. The time saved by this mechanised process meant that many more toys were produced at prices which were easier to afford than those works of art made in the first fifteen years of the century. Tinplate toys became the toys of the masses and it is still possible to find examples made during the 1920s and 1930s in general auctions and antique shops.

A tinplate clockwork battleship 'Maine' by Märklin 54cm (21in) long, *circa* 1904. Sold in February 1989 for £39,600, the world record price for a tin toy!

Novelty toys, made between the wars, were some of the more captivating tinplate toys. They were particularly attractive to children, either because of their droll appearance or unusual mechanical action. Novelty toys came in a wide variety of different types; manufacturers associated with this genre of toy are Lehmann in Germany, Martin in France and Louis Marx in England and America. Many novelty toys represented familiar sights, such as street chestnut sellers or a scratch band, but were given an amusing twist through reducing them in size and providing them with lifelike actions. Created in large numbers at the time, their very popularity ensured that most of them suffered the effects of repeated use. Those that have survived in good condition are widely sought after today by collectors who find their novel actions as appealing today as the children for whom they were originally purchased half a century ago.

A 'Marx Merrymaker's' tinplate mouse orchestra, 17cm (6½in) wide, made by Louis Marx in America, *circa* 1935. Worth £250-350.

Railway sets are the commercially manufactured toys which I am consulted about most often. Whether bought by fathers for their sons or for themselves, it seems to be an English tradition to have an area devoted to a model railway layout somewhere in the house. The German toy factories dominated the British market until after the First World War, after which the companies of Hornby and Bassett-Lowke captured an increasing share of the buying public here. Both factories produced locomotives powered by clockwork and electricity but it was Hornby that accurately assessed the requirements of the purchasers and created sets and individual accessories which were cheap enough to be bought by a child with pocket money. Bassett-Lowke tended to appeal to the railway enthusiast of more substantial means and usually later years than the Hornby pundit.

Unlike other toys, railways were designed to be accurate representations of real-life locomotives and rolling stock; this is very different to the toy vehicles, boats and aeroplanes produced at the same time, which tended to be based on fact but combined with a whimsical quality that made them particularly attractive to children. Toy locomotives, even though generally not built strictly to scale, were designed to represent faithfully known locomotives; some toy collectors miss the whimsical qualities found in other mechanical toys.

It is particularly interesting today to note that the Hornby company has kept pace with childrens' changing interests, proven by the success of their 'Thomas the Tank Engine' range introduced recently. Bassett-Lowke, still in business today, have over the years concentrated their attention on manufacturing scale models.

A Gauge 1 clockwork locomotive 'Sir Alexander', made by Gebrüder Bing for Bassett-Lowke in Germany, *circa* 1904. Worth £600-800.

Toy road vehicles, produced from the 1930s onwards, were also very detailed and made to scale, this time to 1/43rd scale, by the high pressure moulding technique known as 'die-casting'. Originally designed by Frank Hornby as vehicular accessories to brighten up his company's range of Gauge 0 railway, the 'Modelled Miniatures' as they were originally christened were an instant success and it became clear that the six models which were initially produced needed to be substantially increased. The vehicle range was duly augmented and the new styles emerging from Frank Hornby's Meccano factory in Liverpool became known as 'Dinky Toys'. Children found these Dinky Toys

A group of racing and other cars, the largest 18cm (7in) long, made by Schuco in Germany, *circa* 1950. Worth £300-400.

irresistible and it was not long before other manufacturers followed the lead; in England Corgi toys came on to the market in 1956, Matchbox toys in 1953 and Models of Yesteryear in 1956. Abroad other companies produced die-cast vehicles – Tootsie and Manoil in America, and Tekno, Märklin, Solido and Mercury in Europe. Die-cast vehicles are widely and avidly collected today with scarce examples in excellent condition commanding high prices in auctions and specialised shops.

Germany's supremacy in the field of tin toy manufacture was challenged between the wars by other European countries, America and Japan. After 1945 it was the Japanese who expanded quickly in toy production and increasingly used battery power for the movements which in the 1950s and 1960s became more and more complex. The quality of the wares they produced was high and some of the tin cars produced in Japan in the 1950s are faithful copies, chrome trim and all, of some of the most extravagant full-sized American highway cruisers of the time made by companies such as Cadillac, Buic, Chevrolet and Chrysler.

Other aspects of 1950s' and 1960s' technology were reflected by the toy robots and space toys which were produced at the time, stimulated by man's

Below A battery-powered tinplate Chevrolet, 28.5cm (11in) long, made by Marusan in Japan in the early 1950s. Worth £400-500.

exploration of space. These toys combined fact with fiction to form impossible space exploration vehicles and sputnicks together with awesome robot Martians firing sparking death rays from their chests. Although these toys were produced in great quantity at the time, the increasing number of collectors of these toys has encouraged prices to rise quickly and the days of exciting finds at village jumble sales are unfortunately over.

Opposite A tinplate battery-operated 'Attacking Martian' robot, 31.5cm (12¼in) high, with original box, made by Horikawa in Japan in the 1960s. Worth £200-300.

DOLLS

by Hilary Kay

Valuable porcelain, silver or clocks can be admired by everyone although a comparatively small number of people will have known similar antiques in their own homes, but dolls are objects which everybody has either owned themselves or has seen in the houses of older relatives.

WOODEN DOLLS

Although dolls have been found in the tombs of ancient Egypt and in archaelogical digs in Greece and Rome, the oldest dolls which are likely to be found in Britain would date from the late seventeenth century. These dolls' bodies and faces were made of carved wood with well-detailed features to the face. The legs and arms were similarly constructed with pegged joints at the knee, hip and shoulder. The wood was covered with 'gesso' (a paste made of whiting and parchment) then the eyes, lips and colouring were painted on to the face. These dolls are extremely rare and the most valuable are still dressed in the original costume of the period (a pair of these seventeenth-century dolls complete with miniature chairs and a wardrobe of contemporary clothes can be seen in the Costume Hall of the Victoria and Albert Museum in London).

Wooden dolls that are slightly less scarce, although still extremely rare, are those made a century later in the last half of the eighteenth century. If the original costume is still present it is obviously a good clue to the later date of the doll since these dolls have turned-wood bodies and carved faces similar in style to the earlier types. Dolls of this period have wooden legs jointed at the hip and knee. The lower arms are made of wood but with leather or fabric upper arms nailed to the body at the shoulder. Instead of the eyes being painted, enamelled glass was used and a wig made of human hair was nailed to the head.

Fifty years later, in the early nineteenth century, wooden dolls tended to be painted with a highly flushed complexion on the cheeks and, whilst the jointed wooden legs were still retained, the arms tended to be made entirely from kid leather. Some of the most distinctive and easily recognisable dolls from this period were those produced from the Grödener Tal area of Germany.

The twentieth century saw the importation of enormous numbers of so-called 'Dutch' dolls (actually produced in Germany!). These dolls are typified by an oversized head with painted hair and inserted triangular nose, 'mitten'-type hands, and the legs and arms jointed with pegs at the elbows, shoulders, hips and knees. I have sometimes been shown matchboxes from earlier this century entitled 'The Smallest Doll in the World' which contain a tiny version of the Dutch doll; other small versions of the doll were sold as penny toys to be used as Christmas tree or cake decorations. Today these dolls are worth about £20.

A wooden doll dating
from 1760-70, in her
original costume, with
enamelled glass eyes and
real hair wig. Worth about
£3,500- 4,000.

A fine Biedermeier shoulder-papier mâché doll, made in Germany *circa* 1830, 28cm (11in) high. Worth about £400-500.

PAPIER MÂCHÉ DOLLS

The time involved in hand-carving a wooden doll ensured that these could never really be produced cheaply enough to create a mass market. The use of papier mâche, however, did enable dolls' heads to be produced more quickly and more cheaply than those made of wood. Although the earliest papier mâché dolls have been dated back to the middle of the eighteenth century, the period with which papier mâché dolls are most associated is the first half of the nineteenth century. At this time pressure moulding techniques were used to mass-produce dolls' heads with moulded hair in complicated styles, which mirrored contemporary fashion. The fashionable air of the dolls was further helped by their slim bodies and 'Empire' style high-waisted costumes, with which they were originally sold. Their hair and facial features were painted and the one-piece mould of head and shoulders was usually mounted on sawdust-filled kid or cloth bodies, sometimes with carved wooden lower legs and arms. A shoulder-papier mâché doll made in Germany in the 1830s is illustrated and you can see the fine modelling of the elaborate hairstyle and detailed painting of the facial features. Unfortunately, these dolls are fragile and unsympathetic handling has at some stage caused the cracks which run across the collar bone area.

By the middle of the nineteenth century these elegant, fashionable figures were becoming slightly stockier in their style and some were produced without the elaborate, moulded hairstyles which, with the addition of a painted moustache, could be produced as a male figure.

WAX DOLLS

The search for a material which could be easily moulded led to the use of wax as a compound for the manufacture of dolls' heads. Wax dolls can be divided into two distinctive types, those with heads made of wax poured into a mould ('poured-wax') and those with composition heads coated in a thin layer of wax ('wax-over-composition').

The manufacture of poured-wax heads is a process where melted wax is poured into a mould with the desired facial features carved in intaglio and, before the wax has time to set fully, the excess is poured away leaving a thin layer of wax within the mould. Sometimes another application is given in the same way to ensure that the head is thick enough to be relatively robust. After being taken out of the mould, the head is finished by hand, with holes cut for the insertion of glass eyes, the eyebrows and eyelid details are incised, the complexion and lips realistically painted, and hair is inserted.

The English became particularly accomplished at producing good quality poured-wax dolls in the second half of the nineteenth century, the London manufacturers Montanari and Pierotti are especially associated with this type of doll. Although, to the inexperienced eye, both companies produced similar dolls, there are certain differences which indicate one maker or the other if the body of the doll is not marked with the name of the manufacturer. Pierotti inserted hair in the crown of the head into holes made by a hot needle whereas Montanari usually inserted hair into several slits made in the wax with a knife. A poured-wax doll made by Charles Pierotti is illustrated above and shows the quality of facial detail found in the best poured-wax dolls.

A fine Charles Pierotti poured shoulder-wax doll, made in England in the early twentieth century, 53cm (21in) high. Worth about £850.

Moulded papier mâché or composition heads produced in the nineteenth century were extremely attractive but, perhaps, flimsy and not terribly lifelike; dipping the heads into wax gave them a more substantial appearance at an inexpensive cost. Either the composition head itself could be tinted to a flesh tone and then covered with a white or clear wax, or a pale-coloured composition head would be dipped into flesh-coloured wax to provide a more lifelike hue. Like papier mâché dolls, wax-over-composition dolls would have been applied to kid or cloth bodies filled with sawdust; sometimes they would be glued in place beneath the top of the leather body or sometimes sewn to cloth bodies through pre-formed holes in the moulded breast and shoulder plates.

Wax-over-composition dolls were made in England and, to some extent, in America, although the largest numbers of all came from Germany. Motschmann types were produced in Germany in the 1850s. They were an attempt to create a lifelike baby, but the waxed dolls that I see most often are those known as 'pumpkin' or 'squash' heads. These were mass-produced in Germany in

Wax-over-composition 'pumpkin' head doll in original flimsy muslin dress, *circa* 1850. Sold at Sotheby's in 1988 for £135.

fairly shallow moulds and are recognisable by their oversize heads with moulded bright blond hairstyles, usually held in place with a painted ribbon. The illustration shows just such a doll with inserted glass eyes and the flimsy muslin costume in which she would have been originally dressed when sold.

Originally regarded by children as expensive presents, waxed dolls appear to have been generally well looked after by their original owners and large numbers are still in existence. Condition of these waxed dolls is a constant problem, however, because the composition of the head and the wax coating expand and contract at different rates in extremes of temperature and this often results in crazing or cracks to the surface of the head and shoulders. Rough and careless handling can flatten out noses and, of course, dropping a waxed doll cracks the head in a similar way to porcelain.

Original costume is always of particular interest to collectors of dolls as well as adding to the value. Where this is missing care should be taken to make replacements in old, faded, natural fabrics in the correct style for the date of the doll.

CHINA DOLLS

After experiments with papier mâché and wax, the most satisfactory material for moulding dolls' heads (until the evolution of celluloid and vinyls) was found to be china. China heads can be divided into three types: 1. those made of glazed porcelain; 2. those made of untinted unglazed porcelain; and 3. those made of tinted unglazed porcelain.

Glazed china dolls originate mostly from German factories where they were produced in large numbers from the 1840s to the 1920s. They are recognisable by their stark white complexions with dark painted hair, eyebrows and eyes. The bright pink painted cheeks and lips were all covered with an obvious finishing layer of glaze over the decoration. These heads, which were made in one piece with the shoulders, would generally be sewn through pre-formed

A shoulder-china doll, made in Germany *circa* 1880, 71cm (28in) high. Worth about £400-500.

holes on to bodies made of canvas or kid stuffed with sawdust. The china lower arms and legs of these dolls, often with the feet and ankles painted to represent shoes or boots, are extremely vulnerable and were often broken by knocking against each other as the doll was carried about.

The hair of the glazed china dolls was originally merely painted to represent a particular style but, as the nineteenth century progressed, the hairstyles of the doll gradually became more detailed and the styles began to be moulded in china before being painted. The illustration depicts a glazed shoulder china doll from approximately 1880 with an elaborate moulded hairstyle and feathery brushstrokes at the forehead and temples to indicate that the hair has been drawn back from the face.

Unglazed porcelain dolls' heads are normally known as Parian (untinted porcelain) or bisque (tinted porcelain) which were made in a wide variety of different types with great attention paid to detail. Some were modelled wearing necklaces or lace collars and are usually found with elaborate hairstyles, often embellished with moulded and painted ribbons, haircombs and snoods. The eyes of unglazed porcelain dolls are normally painted rather than being made of glass inserted into the head, and the ear lobes are often pierced to take earrings.

In the 1870s manufacturers produced dolls' heads wearing moulded porcelain bonnets or scarves, a novelty which may have been designed to combat the sluggish sales of the more conventional types. The illustration below shows a doll's head moulded with a scarf made by the German manufacturer Alt, Beck & Gottschalck in about 1880.

A fine and rare Alt, Beck & Gottschalck bisque scarf-head doll, made in Germany, *circa* 1880, 32cm (12½in) high. Worth about £600-800.

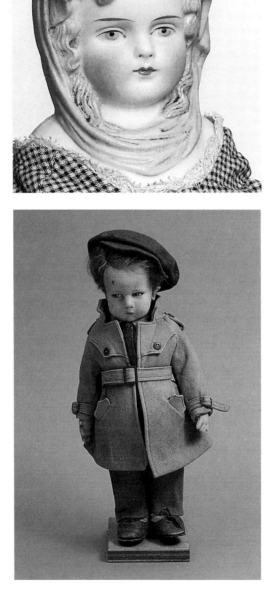

A Lenci felt doll made in Italy, *circa* 1926. Approximately 49cm (19in) high. Worth about £190.

CLOTH DOLLS

As a complete contrast to the sophistication of the moulded porcelain heads, dolls sewn from calico, linen, muslin cotton, felt and velvet were easily made up by mothers at home and have been popular since the nineteenth century. Today, however, it is the commercially manufactured cloth dolls which are of particular interest to collectors.

During the nineteenth century oblong lengths of cloth were produced, machine-printed with the simple outline, features and costume of a doll, ready to cut out, fill and sew at home. Their simplicity and popularity enabled even a child to make her own playmate. Similar lengths of printed cloth are still in production today. These could be classified as the simplest form of cloth doll; the more complex cloth dolls were really imitations in cloth of bisque-headed dolls, with articulated limbs and faces that were well-modelled and three-dimensional.

The maker Kathy Kruse was a particularly successful producer of three-dimensional cloth dolls, commencing production in about 1910 and continuing until the 1950s, although by this time the stockingette faces had been replaced by vinyl. Originally Kathy Kruse dolls' heads were made from three pieces of muslin which were treated chemically on the inside to make them stiff, cut to the accurate shape and sewn, then facial details were hand-painted on to the surface before the head was coated to create a washable finish.

Felt was used as a material for

commercial doll production particularly successfully by the Italian company, Lenci, the English firms of Dean's Rag Book, Norah Wellings and Chad Valley and the Margarette Steiff company in Germany. Felt, when chemically treated to become stiff, can be easily moulded to hold facial features and, with the addition of painted or sewn details, can create an extremely lifelike appearance. In the same way velvet can be used for dolls' heads and the English company, Norah Wellings, is particularly associated with the production of this type of doll. The colour illustration opposite shows a felt doll by Lenci which illustrates several qualities found in most Lenci dolls, in particular the eyes painted glancing to one side, the great care taken in the costume and the hair of mohair sewn directly on to the head.

In the 1920s a fad developed with young fashionable women either to carry a doll when out walking or to use several as decorations in their rooms; the dolls produced to meet this need are generally known as 'boudoir dolls'. Boudoir dolls can be recognised by their stylised facial features and exaggerated eyes and eyelashes which are painted on to the knitted silk or cotton stockingette faces. Although these dolls are not strictly cloth dolls, since the fabric of the face was actually stretched over a moulded composition head, their particular use as adult playthings and fashion accessories rather than actual toys does interest today's collectors.

A good shoulder-bisque swivel-head fashion doll, made in France, *circa* 1870, 46cm (18in) high. Worth about £2,600.

BISQUE DOLLS

However, by far the largest number of collectors are currently interested in the bisque dolls produced by French and German companies from the 1860s until the 1920s. These dolls can be divided conveniently into the French bisque dolls including fashion dolls and bébés, and the German dolls including character faces.

Parisiennes or French fashion dolls were created by the French factories from the highest quality bisque with their features moulded and delicately tinted to resemble a woman of fashion. The bodies of these dolls were made from kid leather with the proportions of a woman, gussetted to allow some movement and filled with sawdust. The best of these fashion dolls are found with their original comprehensive trousseaux which would include shoes, hats, jewellery, undergarments and accessories as well as the costumes themselves. The illustration shows a French fashion doll and trousseau of costume from about 1870 from which her proportions as a fashionable lady are noticeable.

Real human hair wigs in elaborate styles would be either glued to the dome of the head or pinned to a piece of cork inserted into a space at the top of the head. Often the heads would be mounted with a swivelling neck with the bottom end of the neck fitting snugly into a depression of matching shape on the shoulder plate and held in position by a metal rod running through the two.

A fine Jules Steiner bisque doll, made in France *circa* 1880, 58.5cm (23in) high. Worth about £3,300.

French bébés became popular in the 1870s and were unusual in that they were designed to represent children of approximately the age of the owner. Their proportions were essentially childlike and their wigs tended to be long and in simple styles compared with the highly coiffured styles of the Parisiennes produced at the same time. Prior to 1900 the French bébés were produced from extremely fine and delicate bisque with the facial features painted with great skill and detail prior to the second firing. The eyes of these dolls are usually large in proportion to the face. They were made from blown glass with coloured glass threads in the iris which created a particularly lifelike intensity to the eye.

A good French doll of this type, produced by Jules Steiner in about 1880, is illustrated opposite. This example shows some of the other characteristics often seen on bébés of the period; pierced ears, good turned-wood ball-jointed limbs, the pale bisque with an unusual closed mouth and the original pink silk dress.

In 1899 the French doll-making factories combined to form the *Société Français de Fabrication de Bébé et Jouets* to pool their resources and provide effective competition against the flood of bisque dolls produced in the German factories. Generally the French bébés produced after the amalgamation tended to be mass-produced without the attention to detail and hand-finishing, enabling the French finally to compete with the German wares at a similar price level.

In Germany large numbers of factories produced prolifically from the 1870s through to the 1930s (when injection-moulded vinyl dolls' heads became inexpensive and widely used alternatives). I have already mentioned the German Parian dolls' heads which were produced generally earlier in the nineteenth century and the latter part of the century has become associated with tinted bisque heads attached to a neck which fitted into a moulded cup at the top of a composition body, with jointed and moulded composition limbs. German factories usually marked this type of dolls' head with incised initials or a trademark, together with a reference number for the particular face and the size of the body which should fit that size of head.

A group of bisque-headed dolls' house dolls with good moulded detail and wearing their original costume. Made in Germany in about 1890, they stand only 15cm (6in) high. Worth about £150-400 each (would not be sold as a group).

Mass-production techniques ensured that the price of German products undercut those made in France in the nineteenth century and the inventiveness of the German factories in manufacturing different types of doll ensured their pre-eminence in the market. Dolls were produced for particular overseas markets with faces styled as negro, oriental, Indian and other ethnic types as well as so-called 'character' bisque heads.

A bisque doll modelled as a Chinese boy, made in Germany by the Kestner Company in approximately 1914. Sold for £2,860 in 1987.

A good Schonau and Hoffmeister Porzellanfabrik Burggrub Princess Elizabeth bisque doll, made in Germany *circa* 1932, 58cm (23in) high. Worth about £800-1,200.

Character heads were modelled with expressions to imitate real babies and children; sometimes they were made as actual portraits of royalty or children known to the sculptor of the clay or plaster maquette for the original mould. The illustration above shows a character doll which was modelled in 1932 as a portrait of our Queen who was, at this time, Her Royal Highness Princess Elizabeth. These character heads were made in smaller numbers than the conventional dolls' heads and appear on the market less often; as a consequence they are particularly sought after by doll collectors today.

Doll collecting is a popular hobby and fortunately this has stimulated the publication of a large number of books on specific types of doll which I have described in general. If you are lucky enough to own a doll, whether made of wood, papier mâché, wax, china, cloth or bisque, you should be able to find out a great deal about your heirloom and ensure that, by correctly dating it, future generations derive as much pleasure from ownership as you and your family have done.

CLOCKS & WATCHES

by Simon Bull

I would think that very few people leap out of bed of a morning freshly awakened by the ringing of their alarm clock, or, more likely these days, by the insistent buzzing from a quartz radio, and wonder why there are 24 hours in a day. When I was at school I usually wished there were six, but now there are days when I would be happy with 60. Archeology has produced evidence that the day was already divided into a basic 24 hours more than 3,000 years BC, but for the average man in Europe the division of time was of little or no consequence much before 1600; he rose with the sun, and went to bed in the dark. Our reliance upon accurate time-keeping to regulate almost every part of our daily lives is a product of the invention of clocks and watches and their eventual production in such quantities that it is now a rarity to find anyone in the Western world who does not carry a watch.

BRIEF HISTORY OF CLOCKS AND WATCHES

The first mechanical clock was probably invented in the twelfth century and, in common with every other time-keeping device that followed, it required two indispensable parts: some form of motive power and a method of releasing this power at a steady rate. The earliest clocks were driven by weights, usually stones, and the escapement (or controller) by a foliot or balance wheel. The word foliot derives from the French *folier* meaning to dance about in a crazy fashion, and aptly describes the motion of an early clock escapement, all of which were highly inaccurate by modern standards. These first clocks were the property of kings, scientists and of course the church, which dominated all aspects of everyday life. Indeed, early examples, often fitted in churches or monasteries, did not actually show the time but were designed to strike bells to indicate the hours of prayer. And, in fact, the word clock is derived from the latin *Clocca* which means bell.

It would appear that the second invention, so important to making time pieces – the main-spring – occurred in about 1500. This enabled the power to be stored in a portable form, and led to the development of small clocks, watches and travelling time-keepers. The next 450 years were to witness innumerable advances and refinements, many significant and some just plumb crazy, but all making use of these basic mechanical principals.

The Cromwellian lantern clock is an example of seventeenth-century clockwork. It represented an English style that was sufficiently popular to be reproduced from the Victorian era onwards, and to have been extensively faked in this century. Introduced shortly after 1600, original examples were driven by a lead weight, and fitted with a balance wheel and verge escapement. By 1670, the balance had been superseded by a pendulum, and after 1680 the majority of clocks were using a long pendulum with the newly invented anchor escapement. Originally lantern clocks were hung on a spike driven into the cracks between the blocks of stone in a house wall, but the Victorians fitted spring-driven movements into outwardly identical cases and placed them on the mantelpiece.

Original, reproduction or fake: how to tell the difference? If you own a clock like this, then professional advice is a must, as forgeries, particularly miniature examples, have been produced for the past 70 years at least and still appear today. A maker's name can be checked for his working dates, and, although this can of course be faked, the clock should at least show signs of being fitted with the correct escapement for its apparent period. Plenty of vacant holes on the top plate beneath the bell is generally a good sign, as the majority of lantern clocks fitted with a balance wheel or short pendulum were converted to a long pendulum within 50 years of being made. These were the first English domestic clocks and as such were extensively used; therefore indications of wear, damage and replaced parts are likely to be found on a genuine example.

Finally, beware of any lantern clock signed Thos. Moore Ipswich; this innocent clockmaker, who originally flourished between 1720-1789 appears to have been seriously maligned. Whilst visiting an amateur clockmaker's workshop some 15 years ago, I found a whole row of clocks bearing his name lined up on a shelf in various states of disrepair. Apparently exact reproductions were being shipped over from an engineering firm in Eastern Europe, which, after battering and mistreatment, appeared indistinguishable from the real thing. One other point, any miniature lantern clock with a two-core flex coming out of the back – whether fitted with a plug or not – is definitely modern; I have been asked you know!

The longcase or 'grandfather' clock was introduced in the mid-seventeenth century, with the early examples usually London-made and demonstrating the highest levels of craftsmanship both in the movement and the case, which were usually of ebony, walnut or marquetry. To reach the enormous values occasionally reported, that is to say five or even six figure sums, both movement and case must not only be superb quality but also form an original partnership, not a later marriage of components, and be signed by one of the leading makers. The names of Tompion, Knibb, Quare and East come to the mind of most of us in this context, and clockmakers can be loosely divided into divisions, rather like the football league, with the top men making most of the money. If you own a clock signed by a London clockmaker, you are certainly in the upper half!

The average heirloom 'grandfather' clock will, however, date from the late eighteenth rather than the late seventeenth century and be more robust and workmanlike in appearance.

As a general rule, each area of the country is typified by a particular style, and the name on the dial will be in keeping with the type of case. However, it should be remembered that the more successful provincial makers ordered their cases

A late seventeenth-century English brass lantern clock by Edward Stanton of London. Approximate value £2,000.

Left An important pearwood longcase clock by Joseph Knibb of London *circa* 1670. Approximate value £50,000.

Right A provincial mid-nineteenth century mahogany longcase clock with painted dial and striking movement, signed Danen bone, Nottingham. Value £800.

from London, or from top flight local cabinet-makers, such as Gillow. Occasionally a fine case was partially or even totally destroyed by fire or more frequently rot, caused by washing stone floors with buckets of water. If a longcase clock appears to have a disproportionately low base, this may well be the cause, although I have heard of cases being sawn off at both top and bottom to fit into a low-ceilinged room! But it would be untrue to say that masterpieces of English clockmaking have all gone beyond our reach; quite recently a specialist dealer bought in the trade a magnificent walnut clock by Edward East, clockmaker to Charles I: he was offered the clock as being by Edward of East London.

Spring-driven clocks – the most common being mantel and carriage clocks – began to be produced by the end of the eighteenth century. By this time clockmakers had finally mastered the art of making small and accurate main-springs and, combined with the arrival of mass-production in the Victorian age, factories were able to produce large numbers of reliable clock movements at much lower prices. Spring-driven time-keepers became almost as accurate as the 'grandfather' clock, and the latter went into steady decline throughout the nineteenth century.

By far the most frequent types coming to our notice on the *Heirloom* programme are the mantel clock in the marble case and the carriage clock. It is in fact a misnomer to call the cases marble – slate was the far more usual material, being mined in Wales and Belgium, then dyed and polished to give a very presentable finish. Movements were usually French and were mass-produced by several factories, coming in set sizes and supplied complete with

A classic black slate clock, but with a difference. The calendar dials in the centre increase the value by 20 times to £1,000.

the dial and front and rear bezels. They were fitted into cases made in all manner of materials; porcelain, glass, wood and gilt-metal were all popular, but slate was certainly the most commonly used in Britain. Any name appearing on the dial will usually be that of the retailer, not the manufacturer, but it may be possible to establish a date from old trade directories. However, if the same name is engraved on the backplate and the dial, then further research could be worthwhile, as this is more likely to be a much rarer and more valuable English clock. The example I showed on a previous programme, although also in a black marble case, had gilt mounts of top quality, and the movement was signed by Vulliamy, clockmaker to George III, so the value was in fact between £3,000 and £4,000.

A rough guide to the date of manufacture can sometimes be established from punched marks on the backplate of the movement. These are often obscured by the bell, in which case it must be carefully removed. The illustration below shows such an 'award' but do not become too excited: the awards were made at various exhibitions for a particular product and do not refer to your very own clock. Likewise the date given (if any) only proves with certainty that the

View of the backplate of a standard French striking movement, of the type that was fitted into numerous marble, metal and wood-cased French clocks. The bell has been removed to show the award stamp.

movement was not made before the marked year, and could in fact have been made considerably later. The four most commonly found award marks are all of French firms working in the second half of the nineteenth century – Japy, Vincenti, Marti and Pons. Cheaper movements imported from Germany and America were also fitted into many of the mass-produced clocks but even a French example, with an eight-day striking movement and decorated slate case, could be purchased new from £1 in 1900. Matters had improved little by 1970 when the same clock could still be bought second-hand for £1. Here I shall repeat by favourite anecdote about a friend who built an entire garden wall from these cases, after taking out the movements for use as spares. Prices have now risen to £50 plus, but it will probably take 100 years for the cement to crumble away!

Many carriage clocks were actually made by the same factories that produced the ubiquitous marble clock movement, although in fact they were not designed specifically for use in carriages. Throughout the nineteenth century few families could afford to own more than one or two clocks, and the wrist watch was unknown. It was therefore usual for a person to carry a clock from room to room

A group of French nineteenth-century carriage clocks illustrating some of the multitude of popular decorative styles. Values range from £400-1,200.

when required and the carriage clock, being small, was ideally suited for this purpose. Carriage clocks were of course taken on travels and an elderly lady did inform me that she remembered a small window up beside the coachman's seat in their private carriage, into which the clock would be fitted when they departed on a journey.

Two exceptionally decorative French carriage clocks, mounted with French porcelain panels. The porcelain is often claimed to be Sèvres, but although it is in the style of this great French factory, they were in fact made elsewhere. Nevertheless, the value will exceed £2,500 for each clock.

Values vary enormously according to the complication, age and decorative appeal. All carriage clocks were originally supplied with a travelling case in wood and leather, complete with a key and a sliding shutter for the front window, but many have been lost over the years and it has little effect on the price; however, if you are fortunate still to have the box, then keep it regardless of condition. Buyers should be aware that carriage clocks, even quite complicated examples, are still made in France and if artificially distressed and aged can fool the unwitting collector.

American clocks appear frequently among the many photographs sent in to the *Heirloom* programme. As with so many of the clocks that we find in the home, these were again mass-produced in vast quantities. Indeed, by the end of the nineteenth century, production at the leading factories of Seth. Thomas, The Ansonia Clock Company and Chauncey Jerome, to name but three located on the Eastern Sea Board, had reached such levels that clocks were being 'dumped' on the English market, threatening the British industry and leading to questions in Parliament. There are few surprises as the great rarities dating from the early nineteenth century were seldom imported into Britain, so the value depends on condition and the decorative quality of the back-painted glass panel usually featured in the front door.

Pocket watches create another collector's field of enormous scope and variety, but sadly they provide one of the commonest disappointments when it comes to valuations; everybody's favourite heirloom, great-grandfather's watch, or even family treasures going back more than five generations are rarely valuable. Large silver watches with two cases, and known as farmers' or turnip verges, were first introduced in 1820 and continued to be popular in the north of the country until the 1880s. Far more numerous are the 'granny' watches, small silver and gold timepieces, usually engraved, and designed to be worn on a chain or fob. Swiss-made, and costing little more than £2 when new, they are still tucked away in drawers by the thousand. Much the same is true of the larger men's watches, and even a gold case will usually only raise the price by the value of the metal. Frequent advertisements used to appear in a certain weekly paper announcing 'Grandfather's gold watch, gold chain and gold seal for sale – £150'. Undoubtedly somebody's grandfather, but in reality all

Grandfather's gold watch with a difference! Almost identical in shape and size to the typical gold watch handed down through many families, a technical rarity in the movement, known as a Tourbillon, raises its value from a few hundred pounds to more than £10,000.

emanating from the same dealer's stock. He was able to buy 9 carat gold watches, similar chains and mounted gold coins (a coin, if soldered on to a mount, is usually no longer of any numismatic value) for a total of £120 – their scrap value. When the replies came in, out went upwards of ten 'heirlooms' a week – good value, but not really a great investment!

Granny watches par excellence. All these were made in Switzerland during the latter half of the nineteenth century, many by the same factories that produced the simple gold and silver fob watches. These, however, are decorated with jewels, enamelling and delicate engraving. Their values range from £600-1,500.

WHAT TO LOOK FOR

Some features to look out for on watches are as follows: enamel decoration on the case, purity of the gold and the maker's name. On a previous programme we had a 'granny' watch, but enamelled with a pansy flower on the back; although not a great rarity, the value was several hundred pounds instead of £100 or less. English-made gold cases were often in 9 carat gold, but 18 carat was also used and, as well as being twice the value of metal, it was usually reserved for a better quality movement. Continental cases are frequently in 14 carat gold, and the Americans even used a 15 carat standard. Hallmarking laws were strict in Britain, but not always so for the rest of the world, so if in doubt, have the case tested by a reputable jeweller. Finally, any late nineteenth-century watch bearing an English name has a small chance of being a rarity, and it could be worth researching the maker's history.

Looking back over the multitude of clocks and watches that have appeared on *Heirloom*, and the photographs that viewers have sent in, I know that we have not yet found our horological masterpiece. The plain fact is that, unlike many pots, plates and even unsigned pictures, which still lie around unrecognised in people's homes, clocks and watches have always been treasured. The finest examples were expensive when new, and nobody gave away grandfather's gold watch or the longcase clock in the hall to the local church jumble sale; like fine silver, they have tended to remain in the hands of families whose forbears could afford to buy them.

Most of what we have seen on *Heirloom* falls into the groups I have discussed in this chapter – interesting, even puzzling on occasions and certainly quite valuable, but seldom up there with the great pictures discovered from time to time. Nevertheless, four years ago I was reminded of the fact that in the antiques business there is no rule without plenty of exceptions: a family decided that they would sell an old watch, handed down from generation to generation over the years, without any sense of importance. The watch in question had been priced in 1975 by an honourable but non-specialised valuer at £600. When it was sent to me for my valuation what arrived in the post was the most beautiful seventeenth-century watch I have ever seen, and I estimated its worth at a small fortune. The eventual result was quite different; it fetched $1 million, what I would call a large fortune! The illustration can only try to do it justice.

If I had to choose one antique time-piece, I would have to return to the seventeenth century, a period when although watchmakers cooperated with jewellers, enamellers and engravers, there is always a feeling of uniqueness about every piece. Possessing such a watch must have been akin to owning a pair of handmade shoes – a real pleasure!

The world's most expensive antique watch made in Blois, France, *circa* 1660. It must surely have been commissioned for an aristocratic family.

ART NOUVEAU & ART DECO

by Eric Knowles

Art Nouveau is not simply one style but a heading used for several art styles prevalent about 1900. The French treatment of the style is probably the most popularised and has come to represent the Art Nouveau style almost to the exclusion of the equally inventive designs offered by the many talented architects, designers and craftsmen working in Glasgow and Vienna. Even in France the style was subjected to further division with the Nancy school headed by Emile Galle and Louis Majorelle and the Paris school led by Hector Guimard and Eugene Vallin.

The French in general preferred to adopt organic forms into their designs, along with the use or curvilinear motifs and the female form. The posters of Alphonse Mucha best typify French Art Nouveau, making full use of exotically attired maidens imbued with theatrical and ethereal expressions.

The Viennese evolved a style which adopted symmetrical forms and severe lines, sometimes embellished with geometric ornament. The chief exponents were Josef Hoffman and Kolomon Moser, two exceptionally talented designers influenced by their contemporaries in the Vienna Secession – a group or artists and craftsmen who broke away from the 'established' confines preferred by the more traditional members of the Viennese art world. Both Hoffman and Moser had been greatly impressed by the architect and designer responsible for Britain's pavilion at the Turin exhibition of 1902. The designer was Charles Rennie Mackintosh. Mackintosh, along with his three colleagues – Herbert McNair and the MacDonald sisters, Margaret and Frances – were referred to as 'The Glasgow Four' or less affectionately on some occasions as 'The Spook School'. The latter label reflected their use of strange stylised and often shrouded and elongated female forms as integral decoration in their furniture.

The Glasgow Four's style is equally distinctive with an emphasis on perpendicular elements evident in the various tall-back chairs advocated by Mackintosh in many of his commissions for several local wealthy patrons.

Both Glasgow and Vienna provided a strong initial impetus for the design work of the post-First World War era that blossomed as the modern style, and which today we refer to as Art Deco.

Once again, in an attempt to rationalise Art Deco as an art form, it becomes essential to divide the style into two distinct approaches, namely Traditionalist

An Austrian earthenware figure of 'The Butterfly Girl' by the Goldscheider pottery of Vienna. Height 32cm (12½in). During the late 1920s and early 1930s the pottery commissioned figures from several sculptors. This particular example is the work of Lorenzl and the base bears his incised stamped signature. Worth about £500-800.

and Modernist. The former as the title suggests, advocated the use of French decorative design from the eighteenth century and first Empire with the traditional forms given a simplified treatment that made use of exotic wood veneers and ivory. The most famous of the French furniture craftsmen who promoted the traditional approach was Jaques Emile Ruhlman. Ruhlman's work was affordable only by the more wealthy and his clientele often included several maharajahs.

The modernists rejected the ideals of the traditional approach, preferring the materials of the modern world such as steel, aluminium, plate glass and laminated wood. The primary purpose of modernist creations is that of function, with ornament being considered an unnecessary evil to be avoided at all cost. Consequently modernist design sought to combine attractive form with function. The tubular steel furniture of the German designer Marcel Breuer is probably the most typical example of modernist design and one which is still popular and retailed to this day having stood the test of time far in excess of 60 years.

ART NOUVEAU GLASS

A name synonymous with Art Nouveau glass, and which has featured on the *Heirloom* programme on several occasions, is 'cameo glass', and is the work of the French craftsman Emile Galle. Galle's glass may be divided into two distinct groups: the wares made by himself, and the wares mass-produced using industrial techniques. The chances of finding his studio pieces are, to say the least, rather slim, but his mass-produced cameo glass was manufactured long after his death in 1904 until the factory at Nancy eventually closed in 1935.

A Loetz iridescent glass vase, *circa* 1900. Height 19cm (7½in). Only glass made for export was marked, usually with the trademark of crossed arrows or simply Loetz Austria. Value in the region of £500.

It is important to remember that all the mass-produced glass bears Galle's signature, often in the cameo design, and the same signature was used after his death. The post-1904 signatures, however, have an additional small star which was placed as a tribute to Galle's memory.

Not all cameo glass came from Galle's glassworks; indeed, there were literally dozens of other French makers. The most successful glasshouse survives to this day in the form of the Daum factory which, like Galle's glasshouse, is situated in Nancy. It was founded in the 1870s and subsequently run by the two Daum brothers, Auguste and Antonin. The factory usually marked all their wares 'Daum, Nancy', together with the cross of Lorraine motif.

Although cameo glass output at Daum was extensive, I personally prefer the factory's enamelled and etched landscape vases. The variety of such vases never ceases to amaze me – mountain ranges, forests of silver birch, landscapes in snow and even landscapes in rain offer the collector a literally panoramic choice.

The choice afforded by iridescent glass produced in both Europe and America during the Art Nouveau years is probably more expensive than any other type of glass. In the United States the name of Tiffany has become synonymous with the finest examples of both iridescent glass and colourful table lamps. The lamps were usually supported on attractive bronze bases of organic shape, and the shades incorporated glass panels within a bronzed framework which, when illuminated, displayed the design in much the same way as light passing through a stained glass window.

Tiffany's products are marked with a variety of engraved marks, sometimes accompanied by a circular paper label. Once again the collector is advised to exert caution as I recently chanced upon an iridescent vase of dubious provenance which was not only engraved with the initials LCT (Louis Comfort Tiffany) but also had an original paper label – there are no lengths to which the forger will not go.

Dubious signatures have also been known to appear on Austrian glassware of the type produced at the Loetz glassworks. The Loetz factory produced a large variety of iridescent

A Daum-carved overlay table lamp, *circa* 1900. Height 36cm (14in). The applied glass snail visible on the base makes this lamp particularly desirable and consequently expensive, at £30,000.

glass which for years has been considered of secondary importance to that produced by Tiffany. The new collector of Art Nouveau glass is well advised to ignore such prejudices and recognise the obvious virtues displayed by the Austrian craftsmen.

Other Austrian and German glassworks provided iridescent glass similar to that made at Loetz, in particular the glassworks of Pallme König and Habel, and Bakalowitz and Sons. The former are best known for their machine-moulded vases with colour-trailed web decoration; the latter placed more emphasis on shapes using glass of green tint and pale iridescence.

Today's would-be collector of Art Nouveau glass needs to be blessed with a cautious nature when taking into consideration that the marketplace is littered with fakes and improved objects. The improvement referred to usually takes the form of a chipped ruin of a bowl or vase that has been removed in recent times by grinding and polishing, so do beware.

ART NOUVEAU CERAMICS

The pottery and porcelain industries of Britain and Europe all responded to demand for Art Nouveau artifacts by producing decorative vases, tablewares and architectural tilework.

In England the production of Art Nouveau pottery was pioneered by William Moorcroft, who worked as a designer for the Macintyre pottery in Stoke-on-Trent. Moorcroft's early designs were executed in cobalt blue and overglaze iron-red heightened with gilt. The decoration used in these early 'Aurelian' designs was stylised flora of the type popularised in the fabrics and wallpaper of William Morris.

Moorcroft's 'Florian ware' followed and became a huge success employing slip-trailed outlines around Art Nouveau flowers and trees applied to adventurous shapes, often of slender type. The Florian ware pieces all carried the trademark of James Macintyre printed along with Moorcroft's facsimile signature. When the company ceased trading in 1913, Moorcroft set up his own pottery employing many of the redundant Macintyre workers and went on to develop his distinctive range of pottery wares and patterns.

Another notable contribution to Art Nouveau design from a British potter was that of Mintons' 'Secessionist' wares designed by Leon Sdon and Phillip Wadsworth. The range of wares used slip-trailed or tubeline outlines and colourful though often irregular glazes. The influence of the Vienna secession is quite evident and is responsible for the ware being so named.

The Doulton factory at Lambeth produced a large quantity of Art Nouveau-inspired vases decorated by such artists as Frank Butler, Eliza Simmance and Mark V Marshall. The majority of these wares tended to be decorated by junior artists whose marks together with their seniors appear in several specialised Doulton reference books.

Of all the Continental potteries that made Art Nouveau-inspired wares, the Royal Dux factory of Bohemia, now modern-day Czechoslovakia, was probably responsible for one of the largest outputs. The factory produced several types of shell bowl, usually inhabited by mermaids or sea nymphs, that tend to prove the more popular of their Art Nouveau-inspired designs. All items are usually marked with a triangular pad of salmon pink colour impressed with Royal Dux Bohemia, although post-1918 wares substitute Czechoslovakia for Bohemia.

The purist collectors tend to ignore the mass-produced wares of factories such as Royal Dux, in preference for individual artist-decorated pieces, although such items tend to be few and therefore more expensive.

The Rozenburg pottery situated in The Hague is regarded by many as the premier factory producing Art Nouveau ceramics. The eggshell-thin wares are keenly sought by collectors who recognise the hand-painted designs as representing the ultimate in ceramic decoration. As you might expect, such wares are signed with the respective artist's monogram and the printed marks 'Rozenburg Den Haag' above and below a stork emblem.

Iridescence on pottery proved equally as popular as that on glass, and in Hungary the Zsolnay factory at Pecs specialised in producing a whole range of large and small decorative items using this effect. The pottery continued to use such glazes well into the 1920s and the collector is advised to concentrate on the wares of the 1900 period.

In France the Massier family also advocated iridescent glazes. Operating from the Cote D'Azur region, the pottery employed the celebrated artist Lucien Levy-Dhurmer. The signature of Lucien Levy-Dhurmer only appears on items decorated between 1887 and 1895, and Massier iridescent pottery bearing his signature will always be at a premium. All the pottery and porcelain discussed is not beyond the reach of the new collector and is presently turning up at auctions, antique fairs and car boot sales. The collector need not have to part with a great deal of cash to begin a collection if he manages to arm himself with substantial knowledge, tempered with that element of caution.

ART NOUVEAU BRONZES AND METALWORK

Prior to the emergence of the Art Nouveau style, nineteenth-century sculpture had been entrenched in classical, historical and romantic subjects. Many sculptures tended to be of large and sometimes monumental size, affordable only to the

Left A Rozenburg eggshell porcelain vase made in 1906, height 19cm (7½in). Painted by the artist Samuel Schellink, whose monogram together with the year symbol and printed trademark appears upon the base. Worth about £600-800.

A spelter mantel clock, *circa* 1905. Height 43cm (17in). Patinated to resemble bronze, the decorative merits of this clock are questionable. Probably made in Germany or France, it represents a low point in Art Nouveau design. Worth about £200-300.

Left A small bronze match vase and striker designed by Gustave Gurschner, *circa* 1900. Height 8.5cm (3¼ in). Gurschner's signature is clearly visible above the strike panel. Worth about £100-150.

Above A pair of WMF electro-plated on pewter figural candlesticks, *circa* 1905. Height 27cm (10¼in). Five years ago pairs of this type might be purchased for £500-600; today the price is more likely to be £1,200 plus.

Right A bronze bust of an Art Nouveau maiden, *circa* 1988. Height 71cm (28in). Close inspection of this bust reveals poor quality casting and unattractive dark brown patination. Worth about £200.

test is unnecessary on those objects that are stamped with a bronze foundry mark, which usually takes the form of a small medallion. This mark will be found on the reverse of an object around the base.

Many bronze and spelter figures produced during the Art Nouveau period were often functional, taking the form of such objects as electric lamp-bases or a simple paper knife. No item was considered too inconsequential to merit being 'Art Nouveau'd' – crumb scoops, doorplates, inkstands, biscuit tins, seals and matchboxes all succumbed to the Art Nouveau style.

The pewter industry in Britain and

wealthy. During the latter half of the century the popularity of the small bronze continued to grow especially in France and Germany. By the time the Art Nouveau style began to emerge a whole industry was already established producing both bronze and simulated bronze figures. Simulated bronze was usually in the form of white metal or spelter figures patinated or painted to simulate a bronze surface. (Spelter is an alloy of zinc and lead that could be produced for considerably less than bronze.) The simple test in ascertaining whether an item is bronze or spelter is to scratch the metal, preferably under the base; if the colour shows silver the object is spelter, if it is a brass colour, it is likely to be bronze. This

Germany could thank the arrival of Art Nouveau for reviving their flagging fortunes. In Britain the 'Tudric pewter' wares retailed by Liberty's of London's Regent Street followed their successful Cymric silver range. Both the pewterware and the silverware shared the same designer in Archibald Knox, whose distinctive style incorporated strong Celtic elements of design, sometimes embellished with colourful enamel decoration. In Germany the Wurtemburg metalwork factory (WMF), and the Kayserzinn products of J P Kayser all produced decorative and useful wares that incorporated Art Nouveau decoration and form. The WMF wares all bear the tiny diamond shape stamp that includes the trademark of a stork and the initials WMF, whereas 'Kayserzinn' is marked such within an oval panel cast in relief on the base underside of an object.

Yet again new collectors are warned to be on their guard against sophisticated and blatant reproduction Art Nouveau sculpture, usually in bronze although many copies utilise the cold cast method. A cold cast bronze is usually little more than a surface or skin of bronze or bronze-patinated white metal that is given the allusion of weight by being filled with plaster. The collector is advised to become familiar with the feel and look of bronze, and the noise it makes when tapped with another metal object. Bronze will always give a ring, even if of variable resonance, whereas both cold cast bronzes and spelter give out a dull thud.

ART DECO GLASS

The manufacture of Art Deco glass was dominated by France with the glasshouses of Czechoslovakia mass-producing glassware that aped their French competitors. It is the Czech glassware along with minor French and some English factories that the new collector is most likely to come across at flea markets and car boot sales. The better glass tends to appear at auction in specialised sales of twentieth-century decorative arts.

The two French craftsmen whose names are synonymous with 1920s and 1930s Art Deco glass are Rene Lalique and Maurice Marinot. The style of each is a direct contrast of the other. Marinot's production amounted to little more than 2,000 pieces whereas Lalique's production using mass-producing techniques amounted to several million objects. Marinot's work is quite distinctive, with his heavily walled glass vessels encasing metallic foils and air bubbles, and surfaces that emulate the

An opalescent glass figure by Rene Lalique titled 'Suzanne au Bain', *circa* 1930. Height 23cm (9in). Engraved on the base is R Lalique France No 833. No 833 is Lalique's catalogue reference number which refers to his 1932 trade catalogue, in which appears the majority of his productions with relevant photographs and dimensions in metric. Worth about £6,000-7,000.

texture of moss or bark. Rene Lalique's rise to prominence in the manufacture of art glass followed close behind his career as the premier Art Nouveau jeweller. Lalique reproduced the quality of moonstones and opals in his range of glassware known as opalescent glass.

Other French glassmakers such as Sabino, Verlys, Barolac and Hunebelle all included opalescent glass in their catalogues yet none managed to combine the same high quality design and control of opalescence achieved by the Lalique workshops – a quality that can be seen in the colour illustration below of a Lalique scent bottle manufactured for a perfume named 'Le Jade'. The range of Lalique's creations is displayed within the pages of his 1932 catalogue (recently reprinted) and includes glass jewellery, car mascots, vases, figurines and light fittings. The factory signed their wares with several types of signature including relief and intaglio moulded, wheelcut, stencilled and engraved. It is important that the new collector does not confuse the productions of Cristal Lalique, the present day company with that of Rene Lalique. Nearly all the ware produced during Lalique's lifetime (he died in 1945) include the initial 'R' together with the name Lalique.

Another type of French 1930s glass that has featured on *Heirloom* in recent years is that produced using the technique known as pâte de verre. First used by the ancient Egyptians, pâte de verre objects are made by mixing powdered coloured glass with water to form a paste and packing it into a mould. The mould is then heated to a critical temperature whereupon the glass fuses, as opposed to melts, and then allowed to cool before being removed from the mould and trimmed by hand. The best known craftsmen working in this idiom include Almeric Walter, Gabriel Argy-Rousseau and Françoise Emile Decorchemont. Pâte de Cristal figures were made following the same process, the difference being that more lead was added into the paste, which resulted in an attractive glass of less opacity.

Enamelled glass produced during the 1920s and 1930s accounts for a large proportion of art glass output. The collector is advised to look for signed pieces by Goupy, Quenvit, Baccarat and Delvaux. Should the collector come across an enamelled glass vase by Marinot, he could quite easily book a world cruise for two if recent auction prices continue to create records!

A Lalique scent bottle stopper and original presentation carton manufactured for the perfume 'Le Jade' retailed by 'Roger et Gallet'. Height 8.3cm (3¼in). The base is moulded in relief with the initials R L and France. The rare jade green colour combined with the original carton makes this scent bottle extremely desirable. Worth about £3,000-4,000.

ART DECO CERAMICS

In comparison to the Art Nouveau period, the volume of British pottery and porcelain made in the 'modern' style of the Art Deco period was both greater and more inventive. Most of the leading manufacturers produced geometrically inspired decorative items and tablewares. Wedgwood was no exception, calling upon the talents of the New Zealand designer Keith Murray to produce a range of matt-glazed wares that epitomised the machine age. Royal Doulton produced similar tablewares whilst extending their range of bone china figurines to include 'modern' women of the day attired in such outfits as pyjama suits, bathing costumes and fancy dress.

At the Shelley pottery, coffee sets of pure white porcelain, decorated with geometric designs of jade green and black edged with silver lustre, found a ready market and continue to be keenly contested when offered at auction.

The new collector will find a large volume of distinctive wares produced at the Poole pottery of Carter, Stabler and Adams, available today at virtually every flea market. Such volume is usually made up of biscuit barrels, preserve jars, candlesticks and ashtrays and consequently tends to be of small commercial value. Portrait plates are usually the most desirable, and therefore most expensive, of the pottery's productions, being painted in the same palette and depicting stylised faces of the modern woman of the time.

A Royal Doulton bone china figure of 'The Sunshine Girl' designed by Leslie Harradine and produced at their Burslem pottery between 1929 and 1938. Height 12.5cm (5in). The Art Deco ladies produced by Doulton are always at a premium. This particular example is usually priced between £600-900. Collectors are warned to be on their guard against professionally restored pieces. Check necks and exposed limbs for overpainted repairs.

The distinctive palette of Clarice Cliff pottery is presently enjoying an unprecedented return to popularity with prices being paid today in thousands that less than ten years ago would have been in the hundreds.

The vivid primary colours of orange, yellow, black and green applied to the 'Bizarre' and 'Fantasque' range of decorative items and tablewares have also proved irresistible in recent years to the faker. Although such fakes are extremely few and far between, the new collector should remember that all the fakes that have surfaced so far possess an irregular glaze of a pale honey colour.

For as long as I can remember the tasteful designs and shapes found on Susie Cooper pottery have always been regarded as a poor cousin to their Clarice Cliff counterparts. Susie Cooper's designs from the 1930s offer the new collector a real opportunity of acquiring good design at a relatively low price.

In France several Limoges factories, notably that of Haviland, produced geometric tablewares that often bear a close resemblance to those produced by Shelley. Other makers adopting similar decoration include Jean Luce and Marcel Goupy but items by either are rare on this side of the English Channel.

A Clarice Cliff pottery jug from her 'Bizarre' range of wares. Height 17cm (6¾in). The use of bold colour is typical of her products from the mid to late 1930s. Nearly all her production was decorated by the Wilkinson pottery paintresses and few pieces are attributable to her own hand. Worth about £100-150.

ART DECO BRONZE AND IVORY FIGURES

The popularity of the bronze and ivory figure throughout the 1920s and 1930s led to a wide variety of subject matter, the most popular being exotic and long-legged dancing girls by such sculptors as Chiparus, Colinet, Phillipe and Preiss.

Demitri Chiparus was responsible for a whole range of dancing girls, attired in sleek bodysuits, tight bodices, and ankle-length skirts with razor-sharp pleats that echo the science fiction cinema of *Flash Gordon* and *Metropolis*, Fritz

A bronze and ivory figure by Dimitri Chiparus titled 'Le Coup de Vent' (The Squall). Height 31cm (12½in). Dating from the mid-1920s the subject matter would have been considered quite saucy, yet tame in comparison with the figures of Bruno Zach. Worth about £2,000-3,000.

Lang's surrealist prophecy of the future. Chiparus's designs were produced in a wide variety of materials — even tinplate.

Perhaps even more theatrical are the figures of Claire Jeanne Robert Colinet which are dressed in exotic eastern costumes and poised in exaggerated stances upon pedestals of marble and onyx. These pedestals are embellished with a bronze relief panel that is further decorated with hieroglyphics or oriental symbols relevant to that particular dancer of the world.

The figures of Ferdinand Preiss are regarded by many collectors as the ultimate bronze and ivory creations. Many have survived with their original facial tints that imbue each figure with an uncanny lifelike appearance. The wide variety of subjects encompassed by Preiss include classical figures, small children, exotic dancers, golfers, tennis players, bathers and equestrian figures.

The figures of Bruno Zach are by contrast quite single-minded in their pre-occupation with their sometimes erotic and often suggestive subject matter. One such figure caused something of a stir when appearing recently on the *Heirloom* programme. The lady in question was attired in shoes, stockings and a camisole that did nothing to cover her bosom. Both hands were behind her back holding a riding crop, and there was no further evidence to suggest that the lady in question was a lady jockey, but she was certainly a winner with a price tag of over £12,000!

Many bronze and ivory figures were retailed in this country through jewellers, being regarded more as art objects than sculpture. For collectors of limited means many sculptors produced editions in patinated white metal and simulated ivory. The new collector should look closely at the ivory face and limbs for evidence of the ivory grain and any splitting that would prove lacking in the simulated examples of cream-coloured plastic.

The growth in popularity of the bronze and ivory figure during the past ten years has seen the market flooded with modern reproductions, many bearing fake signatures. Familiarity with the original should help prevent failure in recognising such fakes, many of which are stained to resemble age and grime and often have 'over rusted' screws and nuts securing the base.

INDEX

144